GREAT
MALE
DANCERS
OF THE
BALLET

Walter Terry

GREAT MALE DANCERS OF THE BALLET

Anchor Books
Anchor Press/Doubleday
Garden City, New York
1978

The author would like to thank the following for their permission to use photographs: Helen Atlas' Collection, Steven Caras, Anthony Crickmay, Frank Derbas, Fred Fehl, Michael Friedlander, Dwight Godwin, Bob Golby, Hannes Kilian, Francette Levieux, Ralph McWilliams, Mira, Jack Mitchell, Louis Péres, Randolph Swartz, Martha Swope, Linda and Jack Vartoogian; from Copenhagen: John R. Johnsen, Nydtskov, Von Haven.

The line drawings are courtesy of Daerick Gröss.

Designed by Judith Adel

Library of Congress Cataloging in Publication Data

Terry, Walter.
  Great male dancers of the ballet.

  Includes index.
    1. Dancers—Biography. I. Title.
GV1785.A1T39   792.8'092'2 [B]
ISBN: 0-385-04197-7
Library of Congress Catalog Card Number 77–25610

For
TED SHAWN

In memory of the great American dance pioneer who strove, outside the framework of traditional ballet, to make dancing an honorable profession for the American man, and whose dream is at last becoming reality.

Contents

BOYS WILL BE . . . DANCERS!

GREAT MALE DANCERS of the ballet. How many potential ones in the United States of America were aborted by prejudice? Just as Victorian parents blanched at the very thought of a daughter becoming "an actress on the stage" and, thereby, the equivalent of "a loose woman," so American fathers forbade their sons to study ballet since it was presumed to provide a direct path to effeminacy at best and, probably, homosexuality at the very worst. The fallacies of such points of view have become clear today, even laughable if they had not been so tragic. Many great actresses, as wives and often mothers, have proved far more moral than some church choir sopranos; and as the great Vestrises, father and son, sired many children two centuries ago, so have later male ballet stars, Youskevitch, Nagy, d'Amboise, Villella, Kehlet, Eglevsky, Massine, among many, produced progeny. But, as in all other walks of life, there are all kinds of life styles and moralities.

With the first stirrings of "women's lib" in matters of politics, economics, and social structure came comparable stirrings of a new style "men's lib" with respect to the arts. In the 1920s, if a boy postponed getting a haircut and his hair was a trifle long, his father would likely snort, "Planning to take up the violin?" Violinists, musicians, poets, and, indeed, all artists were referred to as "long hairs," a derogatory term indicating that the arts were derogated too as being pretty awful for "a real boy." Dancing? A flicked wrist and a sneer said it all.

For American boys—straight, gay, or asexual—any indication of interest in the arts, other than a brief period of "taking piano," learning a band instrument, or singing in a choir or glee club,

Male dancer in drawing showing the musculature as he leaps into the air, doing a *grand battement*, or kick to the front, or *en avant.*

Male dancer standing in the position known as *à la seconde*, with the leg raised *en haut*. This is one of the variations on the five positions of the feet, with comparable positions of the arm. In this one the leg is *à la seconde*, extended; the arms are in second position also.

Examples of *batterie*, the beating of the legs in flight. These are *cabrioles en arrière*, leg beats to the back as the dancer moves through space.

A *grand jeté*, with the arms in first position.

could bring down paternal wrath or, at least, hurt disapproval. Mothers were better. Knowingly or instinctively they tended to protect what the great dance pioneer Ruth St. Denis referred to as "the divine androgyne" in their sons, just as fathers tried to instill something of the sports*man* in their daughters.

In the first half of this century, if an American boy wanted to study dancing, he had two hopes: (1) to go to ballroom dance class where he could learn "steps" to do at the prom with a girlfriend when he was old enough to have a girlfriend or, stretching a point, (2) to take some tap dance lessons. For a long time, the route to ballet lessons was via a tap dance class. If a lad attended a studio where toe, tap, ballet, acrobatics, and baton twirling were taught, he could sometimes sneak from his tap class into ballet, usually with the encouragement of a ballet-oriented instructor. Hopefully, Daddy would be none the wiser.

Truthfully, in many small towns, boys who felt drawn to dance were not necessarily drawn instantly to ballet. They may never, pre-television, have seen any ballet. They went to movies. They saw Fred Astaire and Gene Kelly. The boys had rhythm, they were athletic, and the two, combined, were what Astaire and Kelly did. What was wrong with that? Later, as the youngsters' horizons extended, ballet exposure would come along and then a decision had to be made. In most cases, if ballet was opted, the boy's decision was at odds with his father's wishes. The choices were to take ballet lessons on the sly and hope not to be discovered, to brazen it out and say "or else," or to leave home at sixteen and make it by washing dishes, mopping down studios, doing some show biz if possible while studying ballet assiduously. Careers in ballet were born this way. More fell by the wayside because they gave up or because they started too late.

Parental approval, if it ever came, was based, as far as fathers were concerned, on the physical rather than the esthetic attributes of dance. When I began my studies, at college age, in the 1930s, my father, who had fortunately been accustomed to theater all his life, although a businessman himself, tried to dissuade me from my dance studies when I had written home about my

A *grand jeté* with the arms high over the head, in another ballet position.

A *grand jeté* with the arms in still another position.

first classes. Home on vacation, I showed him some of the classwork. He looked surprised and then said, "That's very good exercise, very good." I had little further trouble. A college friend actually joined, on graduation, a dance company (modern dance) and was terrified but hopeful when he knew his father was coming to a performance. (His brother had played college football and gone into business—this the almost universally approved pattern for the American male—and he had to compete with that image.) After the program, his father came backstage to see his "errant" son, who was standing there drenched in sweat. "Well, son," he said, "you certainly worked hard." That too was a sort of ap-

proval. Both parents, and thousands of others, would respect anything that showed the muscle, the stamina, the grit, the butchness of their male child. The physical side of dance could do that.

Matters parental and, especially, paternal, are better today but they are by no means ideal. Sons of teenage are permitted to take classes in gymnastics. That's masculine, isn't it? They can even do their gymnastics to music. That's called "rhythmic gymnastics," isn't it? Okay. But give that boy exactly the same routine and call it "dance" and you're in deep trouble. The American prejudice against dancing for men, though disappearing, runs deep.

European boys rarely experience such prob-

A *grand battement* to the front with the arms in the third position, and a jump, a *sauté*.

Those accepted enter the Royal Danish Ballet. Peter Martins, now a *premier danseur* of the New York City Ballet and a frequent guest in his nation's Royal Theater, was an enormously gifted pupil as a child. I watched him, when he was ten years old, in a boys' class in the old studio where the bust of August Bournonville, Denmark's greatest choreographer of the last century, looks down on succeeding generations.

Peter was at *barre* and doing well in a ballet style which, for a century, had been particularly compatible to boys who dance. I asked my photographer companion to take his picture. "Why him?" I was asked. "Why not one of the other boys?" I answered, "Because that one is going to be a star." Some years later, when Peter joined the New York City Ballet, he told me he almost ruined my prediction. "I got to hate dancing," he said. "When I reached my teens, I didn't have a life like other boys. I wanted to quit and go into sports." But he stuck out the transitional period of rebelliousness, to become a devoted, dedicated servant of dance, to become a star. Perhaps his son, now studying ballet, will follow in his footsteps.

In Imperial Russia and today in the Union of Soviet Socialist Republics, the pattern for state theaters is the same as in ancient Denmark. Boys as well as girls, at the age of nine, apply for entry into the state schools in more than fifty Soviet cities. They are examined as carefully as in Denmark and they too have their total academic education right along with their ballet training, as do the students of drama or music. Rudolf Nureyev, born in Siberia, found ballet training available to him in a village near the Urals.

In Europe, it has always been this way. True, during the 1800s and the early part of this century, there were many fewer male-child applicants than today, but not because of a fear that dancing was wrong for boys but because there was precious little opportunity for them in a century-and-more during which the female totally dominated the art, the act (and the business) of dance. Then, too, one must remember that Europe has had dance family dynasties, famous ones in which sons and daughters followed in

lems. In Denmark, with the oldest, continuously functioning royal ballet in the world, both boys and girls are auditioned every year at the Royal Theater in Copenhagen. The kids are seven or eight years old, they are examined by doctors, they are tested by ballet instructors, and if they are accepted they enter the Royal Theater and may, very possibly, stay there for the rest of their working lives and retire on a pension that gives them splendid security. Of course, some students fall by the wayside because of lack of interest or lack of talent. The gifted ones, as aspirants, must later pass rigorous tests at graduation time.

A see-through diagram of how the male lifts the female
and what her body does as he stands behind her.

their parents' dancing footsteps. Such dynasties
continue to this day. Even at the start, America
had a dancing theatrical family in the Durangs,
for John Durang, son of a soldier of the American Revolution, became our first major ballet
dancer, and members of his family continued the
tradition until the woman of the ballet usurped
all male rights in ballet even to the point of sub-
stituting herself in male roles.

But in America, the male is slowly being liberated today from the bonds of prejudice against a
career in dance. And because of it, America is beginning to produce, late in its cultural develop-

ment, some of the great male ballet dancers of
the day. Belated it may be, but the American boy
had problems bucking parental prejudice and
downright forbiddance that a great French
dancer of three centuries ago did not face. At six
years old, this Frenchman was pretty much his
own boss. His father was dead, so he didn't have
to ask his approval (although his father had enjoyed the dance), and his mother was more concerned with politics and guiding him in such
matters. So he did as he pleased and he danced
throughout most of his life. He could because he
was King. He was Louis XIV.

2

KING
OF DANCERS
AND THREE
DANCING
GODS

The world's first ballerina, Lafontaine, made her debut in Paris in Lully's *Le Triomphe de l'Amour* on May 16, 1681. Such was her own *triomphe* that she was instantly hailed as *"première des premières danseuses"* and accorded the title *reine de la danse*. In the three centuries of professional ballet between Lafontaine and Margot Fonteyn, the reigning monarch of classical dance has almost always been a woman, the ballerina, the *reine de la danse*. But before there was a Queen of the Dance in France, there was a King. For it was Louis XIV who caused the establishment in 1661 of l'Académie Royale de la Danse. This was primarily a deliberative body of dance experts whose duty it was to raise the standards of the art. In 1669 the King founded l'Académie Royale de la Musique and, in 1672, ordered his great composer, Jean-Baptiste Lully, to incorporate a school of dance, specifically for the training of pupils, within the framework of this academy. Thus, the purposes and functions of the two academies were combined to form the ancestral structure of today's Théâtre National de l'Opéra.

Why should this particular King of France concern himself with ballet? Because His Majesty was a dancer as well as a ruler. He was, in fact, the first dancer of the realm. Appropriately, a title associated with him throughout history, Le Roi Soleil (the Sun King), does not refer simply to the splendor of his Palace of Versailles or his

Print, King Louis XIV in Carrousel costume for an equestrian ballet.

(Overleaf) Print, scene from *Giselle*.

resplendent reign, but to a role he danced in court ballets, Apollo, the Greek sun god. The court saw Louis as Apollo in *Les Nopces de Pelée et Thétis* (1654) and in *La Nuit,* and although he played Jupiter and Neptune and other gods and heroes, Apollo was his favorite role, for it suited, artistically, esthetically, and politically, the Sun King himself.

There were, of course, other male dancers, both courtiers and professional performers, to be seen during the long (1643–1715) reign of Louis XIV, but the King was an ardent, tireless, and dedicated dancer. Not only did he portray the mighty gods of Olympus but he also enjoyed playing the part of a buffoon or even a crook. He danced, of course, in the ballets composed by Lully, his composer, and by Pierre Beauchamps, his ballet master and principal choreographer, but he also participated in some of the comedy-ballets by one of the greatest playwrights, Molière. When necessary, Louis sang as well as acted and danced.

How good a dancer was Louis XIV? It would be difficult to say. But one thing is certain: His Majesty never received a bad review!

Until the advent of Lafontaine and her colleagues, professional dancers were almost always male. True, the ladies of the court, from the Queen right down the social scale, danced, but in the public areas of entertainment young boys danced the roles of girls, just as in England boys were the heroines in Shakespeare's plays. But with Lafontaine, the male dancer slowly receded in importance. Not all at once, but as the King withdrew from demanding dance roles, ballet would not see another supreme King of Ballet for nearly three hundred years, when Lafontaine's descendant, Fonteyn, chose Rudolf Nureyev, newly defected from the Soviet Union, as her partner. First, he was her youthful consort; then, as she withdrew from performing ballet's great classics, Nureyev became the greatest box office attraction in all ballet, the superstar, the King of Dance.

Between the two kings, however, are generations of great male dancers, some barely surviving the almost total dominance of the ballerina in the nineteenth century. All of them had to settle

Print of Balon, an early dancer who gave his name to the term *ballon,* which means "lightness of feet."

for being Prince Consort to the ruling Queen of the Dance, but some of these consorts exerted tremendous influence on their partners and, as in the case of Vaslav Nijinsky, on the whole world of ballet.

If Louis XIV shared his supremacy, in ballet as well as in power politics, with no one, he did share his stage with other male dancers. Lully, a dancer as well as composer-conductor, would oc-

Lestang, an early dancer.

Gaetan Vestris, the first of
the great family, an actor-dancer.

Jean-Georges Noverre, the great choreographer and reformer, who worked with Vestris and had his collaboration.

casionally correct the King in performance as he danced with him. And as for Beauchamps, it was he who conducted the classes that produced the first professional dancers—Lafontaine among them—codified steps and patterns into a teaching method, and actually invented a simple system of dance notation which could serve the dance needs of the time. His skills as a choreographer, teacher, pedagogue, notator are undisputed in the annals of dance history. As a dancer, it was said that he was wanting in stylishness but that he made up for this lack with the fire and vigor of his movements and with his excellence in turns. *Pirouettes* were developing in the 1680s and there is reference to Beauchamps executing a *tour en l'air*.

Beauchamps was followed in the male wing by Louis-Guillaume Pécourt, described as a *demi-caractère* dancer but one noted for his lightness and for a versatility that included not only com-

mand of various styles but also of the art of mime. Pécourt was also a great dancing favorite of the ladies. His co-*premier danseur*, Louis L'Etang (or Lestang), on his retirement established a successful dance school of his own. Pécourt's lightness, or *légèreté*, was matched and, apparently bettered, by Jean Balon (or Ballon) whose name, *ballon* entered the vocabulary of classical ballet itself as the standard term to describe the bouncing quality, the elasticity, the resilience of a dancer demonstrated during leaps or jumps or any aerial actions. His *légèreté prodigieuse* was not all he had to offer. He was a superb actor-dancer and it was he who was the mime partner of the great ballerina Françoise Prévost in the first ballet-pantomime to be played in France (1708), in which the two mimed the final act of Corneille's play, *Les Horaces*, as a highlight of a fête given by the Duchesse du Maine in Sceaux. The event, a historic one in dance, was described by one viewer: "They vitalized their gestures and the play of facial expression to such a degree that they caused tears to flow."

Ballet during the reign of Louis XIV was not at all like ballet today. It was truly opera ballet, for productions included singing, speaking, recitatives as well as dancing. And the dancing usually consisted of various *entrées*, perhaps as many as twenty or thirty, but not performed in sequence as we would find in later ballets. Dancing, actually, had been introduced into opera by Lully because the French disliked opera. Ballet was the bait to get them to attend, or enjoy, Italian opera.

Thus, it was something of a shock for an audience to see dancers "act" in gesture a part of a play normally expressed through the spoken word or, in opera, in song. But ballet then and now differed in still other ways. Lafontaine, Marie-Thérèse Subligny (her successor), and Prévost all wore shoes with heels, corsets, petticoats, panniers, skirts that reached the floor, elaborate headdresses. That they moved, let alone danced, is something of a minor miracle.

The men were less encumbered. But Louis wore heeled shoes and so too, at least at first, did Balon and his equally famous male colleague

Gaetan Vestris' son, Auguste Vestris, considered the greatest male dancer of his day.

Michel Blondy (or Blondi), a nephew and a pupil of Beauchamps. The two, exactly the same age, joined the Opéra in exactly the same year (1691) and their rivalry gave the public the same titillation and excitement that would be echoed centuries later with, say, Anton Dolin and Serge Lifar, André Eglevsky and Igor Youskevitch, Rudolf Nureyev and Mikhail Baryshnikov. At the time, it was said that Blondy was "one of the most beautiful dancers to be seen . . . the greatest dancer in Europe . . ." and that Balon, in addition to his "lightness," possessed "an expressivity without precedent . . . a tender air especially apparent in *pas de deux*."

Blondy and Balon, Beauchamps and Pécourt, the near acrobatic Molière (who performed *commedia dell'arte* style in his own comedy-ballets), and even Louis XIV himself were freer to move than were the ladies. Their legs were stocking-covered only right to the upper thigh, unless a role called for an unusually fanciful costume, the shoes had low heels and, very often, almost no heels at all, and the upper body was clad in a doublet-style coat or jacket. In essence, the male dancer's dress was the courtier's standard "doublet and hose." Thus, Molière could execute a fairly spectacular high kick to the rear and Beauchamps could propel himself into a *tour en l'air*, a male movement which he invented. As a virtuoso of ballet, the male was dominant. It was he who did *pirouettes* and leaps and *grands battements*. The lady was grounded. True, there are references to *entrechats* and *cabrioles*, but they would have been done close to the floor and under the vast hoopskirts. It would have been almost impossible to see them. Marie Camargo changed all that and initiated the removal of the male dancer from his supremacy.

Camargo, who made her debut at the Opéra in 1726, had been first a pupil of Prévost, the reigning ballerina, until the newcomer replaced her senior in the adulation of the public and in the affection of Prévost's favorite partner Blondy. Two men of the ballet aided the teenage Camargo in her battle for stardom and in her unintentional efforts (or were they?) to achieve equality with the *premier danseur*. Prévost, in a fury, ceased her teaching of young Marie and had her removed from a position of soloist to the back row of the *corps de ballet*. Blondy fell in love with Camargo and became her teacher, introducing her to his own mastery of male dance steps. At a historic performance, David Dumoulin, a brilliant dancer, failed to make his entrance for a Demon Dance—was it by accident or on purpose?—and Camargo, dashing from the back row to stage front, improvised a solo to the demon music. Her triumph was instant and complete. (Prévost, shortly, retired.)

Camargo, a brilliant pupil of a male teacher and a brilliant pinch-hitter for an absent male dancer, decided to move a step further toward dominance. Observing the men's freedom of the limbs, she shortened her skirt to just below the calf. It shocked Paris. But it permitted the public to see Camargo's *batterie*, the leg beats at which she excelled, for if she did not invent the *entrechat* (some say she did), she certainly brought it to a new peak of perfection. Wanting to increase her spring, her *ballon*, she removed the heels from her shoes and, very possibly, invented the ballet slipper.

Up to this point, the ballerina had been principally a *terre-à-terre* dancer, hidden *entrechats* to the contrary. Camargo lifted her into the male dancer's domain, the air. Researches by the late Lillian Moore, one of the great historians of ballet, led her to believe that "in Camargo's dancing there was a certain strength and virility that was almost masculine, a quality that never before had been seen in the work of *danseuses*." Marie Camargo, then, narrowed the gap between the technique of the male and the female dancer. Still, male prowess remained greater than that of the female by nature's own plan. Only the unnatural toe shoe (yet to be invented) would give the ballerina her edge over the male.

The *danseur*, then, had a few more years of dominance left to him. The female may well have earned the title *reine de la danse* upon the occasion of her celebrated debut as a professional dancer in 1681, passing the title on to her successors, but she was soon to be outranked by a man who made his dancing debut at the Opéra in 1714, just as the Sun King's reign was drawing to a close. His name was Louis Dupré. Almost instantly he was called *le grand Dupré* because of the majesty of his bearing and the nobility of his movements, but in due course he was elevated still higher and upon him was bestowed, by popular acclaim, the title *dieu de la danse*. One can't go much higher than that.

Admirers waxed poetic about Dupré: "One could believe that he witnessed a god step down from the altar in order to mingle in the dances of mere mortals." Jean-Georges Noverre, the great ballet master, choreographer, and reformer of the mid-1700s, recalled Dupré as being "a beautiful machine, perfectly organized but lacking a soul. His rare qualities ascribe to him a celestial air. But he is always uniform. He never varies in a dance and he is always Dupré." But Dupré, whatever his faulty faultlessness, is important to the heritage of the male dancer. *Noblesse* was much admired, for dancing, one must remember, was the pastime of kings and especially a great King, Louis XIV. Nobility in movement was cultivated by all male dancers and *le grand Dupré* carried it to perfection and was the model for the *premier danseur noble*, a very special rank, rather like that of the *prima ballerina assoluta*, that are bestowed on few dancers. In our time in the twentieth century, Erik Bruhn was a great *danseur noble*, bequeathing the crown to Ivan Nagy.

Even when Dupré was nearing sixty, his art and his popularity appeared to be undiminished. The great lover Casanova saw him and marveled. "I was astonished," he wrote, "and I asked my companion why." His friend, a longtime Dupré follower explained, "One applauds the grace of Dupré and the divine harmony of his movements . . . his perfection has always been absolute, yet each time we see him we believe we are seeing that perfection for the first time."

Dupré retired in 1751, relinquishing the post of first dancer at the Opéra to his pupil Gaetan Vestris, who soon was hailed as *le dieu* (or *diou*, in that period) *de la danse*. There were to be three dance *dieux* in all, with Gaetan's son, Auguste, the last. Gaetan, born in Florence in 1729, ruled supreme from the time of Dupré's retirement in 1751 until his own farewell in 1782. There were, of course, hiatuses, for Gaetan became involved in numerous love affairs complicated by duels,

and his own arrogance was not always countenanced by those in higher place. That arrogance, however, could be amusing. Once, when a hefty lady trod on his foot and apologized profusely, he said, "You have simply put all of Paris into deep mourning for a fortnight!" He once said that there were three great men in the world, Voltaire, Frederick the Great of Prussia, and himself. The year before his retirement, he and his son danced together in London and such was their fame and stature that Parliament did not sit that day in order that its members could attend the performance.

Gaetan, inarguably, was as talented as he was vain. He continued the tradition of the *danseur noble* established by Dupré. Most surely he enlarged the technique of the male dancer—his wife, the German ballerina Anna Heinel, invented *pirouettes à la seconde*, a step destined to become a tour de force for the *danseur*—not only because of his association with his masters and his colleagues in an expanding theatrical era, but also because of his own natural prowess. Finally, he was a superb mime. This quality, added to his own quest for a variety of roles, led to a major innovation in ballet performing. His vanity also played a part in this matter. Dancers, at that time, were masked. There were a variety of masks for different roles, different moods. Acting eloquence was possible only through gesture. Noverre, the reformer of choreography, a pupil of Dupré as was Vestris, envisioned a new form of ballet. He called it *ballet d'action* and it was predicated upon the concept that movements should have meaning, that they should forward dramatic action. Noverre's revolt was against ballet which existed only to produce bigger and better *cabrioles*, *entrechats*, and other feats of skill.

Ballet was mainly *divertissement*. It highlighted opera performances but it did so chiefly through elegance and virtuosity. Noverre, strongly impressed by the choreography of Camargo's contemporary Sallé, the ballerina who accented dramatic action, and greatly influenced by the distinguished English actor David Garrick, brought to ballet the concept of dance-drama. The mask, he felt, was only a feeble prop and he found himself fascinated with the way that Gar-

A print of Armand
Vestris (son of Auguste)
with Mlle. Angiolini.

rick used paint, greasepaint, or makeup to establish a facial character while leaving the face itself mobile. He was met, of course, with total disapproval of his reform attempts with respect to *ballet d'action* and the discarding of the mask. Indeed, Paris would have none of it. In order to fulfill his dreams, he left Paris and it was at Stuttgart, at the ducal court of Württemberg, that he was able to experiment. Here he worked from 1760 to 1767 and here he wrote one of the major ballet books of all time, *Lettres sur la Danse et sur les Ballets,* setting forth his principles. Gaetan Vestris came to Stuttgart to dance for Noverre and because of both his vanity—a desire to show his face on stage—and a belief in Noverre's art, he performed without a mask, possibly the first major dancer to do so. The ballet was Noverre's *Médée et Jason* (Stuttgart, 1763).

Auguste Vestris, the third "god of the dance," was the illegitimate son of Gaetan and the leading ballerina of the Opéra, Marie Allard. Indeed, he was sometimes called Vestr'Allard. The fact that he outshone his own dazzling father in no way upset the senior. In fact, the father was pleased and explained it by saying that Auguste had one great advantage that he, Gaetan, had not; that was that Auguste had Gaetan for a father!

Auguste, born in Paris in 1760, made his first big success at thirteen in a ballet created by his father, who was ballet master and, briefly, principal choreographer as well as first dancer at the Opéra. At sixteen Auguste was appointed soloist, at eighteen he was a *premier danseur,* and at twenty he was the star of the troupe. He lived to be eighty-two years old, long enough to witness the decline of the male dance and the omened oblivion. He retired in 1816 but appeared at seventy-five in a gala as partner to Marie Taglioni, the ballerina who ushered in the Romantic Age of Ballet, who made the ballerina supreme, who ruled as "queen of the dance" and set the pattern for the male dancer to be nothing more than a consort (at best) for nearly a century.

During his dancing career, Auguste Vestris was viewed not only as the first dancer of the Paris Opéra but also as the first dancer of Europe. His elevation was breath-taking, his *batterie* something to marvel at, and his pirouettes were said to be unequaled. London adored both Vestrises. And in 1786, one critic reported of Auguste, "He rises four feet," and in 1793, another compared the turning prowess of three dancers, relaying the information that Nivelon could do only four *pirouettes,* Dauberval anywhere from five to eight, and the great Vestris a minimum of six but usually eight. Louis Nivelon, of a much earlier generation, had come to London as early as 1707 and organized a company. His son, Francis, continued the dancing tradition. Jean Dauberval, a dancer

Print, Pierre Gardel, a contemporary of Auguste Vestris'.

of great distinction, is known to posterity as the choreographer of *La Fille Mal Gardée*, the great comedy classic created in 1789 and often regarded as the oldest ballet extant in twentieth-century repertories.

But if Auguste Vestris had a rival, it was not Dauberval or Charles LePicq (Noverre's favorite pupil, described by Noverre as "This Proteus of the dance who unites in himself every style"), but Maximilien Gardel, a brilliant technician and himself an innovator, for although Vestris senior had discarded the mask at Noverre's behest in Stuttgart, Gardel was the first to dance maskless (1773) in Paris at the Opéra. He and Dauberval succeeded Noverre as joint ballet masters and choreographers at the Opéra (1781). His younger brother and pupil, Pierre Gardel, succeeded him not only as *premier danseur* but also as chief choreographer and ballet master. In addition, he came to head the ballet school. So from 1787 until retirement, he ruled supreme, surviving revolution and countless government changes until his death in 1840.

But Vestris had one other rival, twenty years his junior, Louis Antoine Duport, whose dancing at the Opéra from 1797–1808 has been described as "sensational," "phenomenal," "incredible." He choreographed also, and successfully. But he was arrogant, greedy, and contemptuous of authority, even that of the Emperor Napoleon, and eventually was forced to flee Paris disguised as a woman and accompanied by a former mistress of the Emperor! He journeyed to Russia, where audiences went wild for him, his virtuosic *pirouettes*, his legendary lightness. He was especially admired in the ballets choreographed by Charles-Louis Didelot, a Swedish-born pupil of Noverre who had brought Noverre's concept of *ballet d'action* to St. Petersburg and who laid the groundwork during his years there (1801–11 and 1816–37) for the great school of ballet that would become the training ground for the superstars of Russian ballet from the Maryinsky through the Kirov.

Duport was the toast too of Vienna, Naples, London, and elsewhere in Europe. But did he come to America? There is a mystery here, for a brilliantly gifted child dancer named Louis Duport did indeed dance in America in the early 1790s. But could he have been the great Duport from Paris? Remotely possible despite conflicting dates but Lillian Moore came up with another theory by way of compounding a fascinating mystery. The young "American" Duport, following a performance in Savannah, Georgia, in 1796, set forth for Charleston, South Carolina, where he had performed earlier. He never reached his destination. He was never heard of again. Miss Moore posed the fascinating theory that he might possibly have been the Lost Dauphin of France, the son of Louis XVI and Marie Antoinette who disappeared when the royal couple were guillotined. Certainly, the heir to the French throne had studied ballet extensively. His mother, as a child at the imperial court in Vienna, had studied with Noverre and had been instrumental in having Noverre appointed ballet master at the Opéra in spite of violent institutional opposition. So the Dauphin was most surely a skilled and "noble" dancer and if Master Duport were indeed the Dauphin, it might well have occurred to French revolutionaries that a pretender to the toppled French throne should be removed permanently from the scene. Could it be that a kingly dancing heir to the great Louis, the Sun King who started it all, was not permitted either his balletic or political inheritance?

Between the two Louis, if indeed Master Duport were the missing Louis XVII, between two kings of the dance, the male dancer in ballet remained supreme throughout the entire eighteenth century. Not even Lafontaine or Prévost, Camargo or Sallé could displace three "gods of the dance," Dupré and Vestris *père et fils*, and of them all, perhaps Vestris *fils*, the son of the great Gaetan, was the incomparable. Miss Moore writes of a delightful commentary unearthed in her researches. Two gentlemen, gasping over the unbelievable elevation of Auguste Vestris, made awed comment. Said the first, "How light he is! He must live on a diet of butterflies." Replied his companion, "No, he eats only their wings."

3

"UGLY AS SIN" BUT A SUPERSTAR

THE MALE DANCER, during the nine-teenth century when the ballerina was not only a *reine de la danse* but also deified into a *déesse*, was usually the consort, frequently little more than a *porteur* and more than occasionally nonexistent. Once the ballerina had elevated herself onto *pointe*—just about the only non-male area of special prowess open to her—the way was prepared for a new accent on technical development. The dancer had gone just about as far (so they thought at the time) as possible with *pirouettes* (Vestris the younger had done eight), *cabrioles*, and the like. Dancing on toe was more than a fad. It was a challenge to choreographer and teacher as well as to the female dancer. Thus, ballet technique took a new turn, and since men did not dance on toe and could not do so easily because of their heavier weight, except in rare character assignments, the technique of ballet, or its style at least, shifted to the distaff, or female, side.

The male dancer remained to support the ballerina when she was perched perilously and sometimes precariously on *pointe*. He was there to lift her, for the mere act of rising onto toe invited a still higher excursion into space, and it was the male, through the strength of his arms and back, who could lift his sylph, dryad, wili, nymph, or fairy of some sort from her self-propelled *relevé* to the higher reaches of aspiration and fantasy *en l'air*.

(Overleaf) Saint-Léon, playing a violin. He made his debut as a musician in 1834 and as a dancer in 1835. He is shown here with his ballerina wife, Fanny Cerrito, in a ballet.

Toward the middle of the century, the unkindest cut of all occurred when female dancers began to perform male characters in ballet. Oh, yes, genuine males were required for support of the ballerina but they did not need to dance. They could lend acting skills and muscle to the performance. The role of Franz, in the great comedy-ballet *Coppélia*, was first danced by a female dancer *en travestie*. The first prima ballerina of the Metropolitan Opera House at its opening (1883), Malvina Cavalazzi, was especially famous for her interpretation of male roles. So it was that in the 1800s, the *premier danseur* was neither a king nor a god; he was either a porter or he was nonexistent.

There were exceptions to this sorry state of affairs. The major exception was a very, very short man with a face "as ugly as sin" (so described by one of his colleagues), Jules Perrot. Here was one of the great male dancers of the century, perhaps the greatest of them all.

A critic of the day wrote of Perrot, "he alone has survived the great reform which has just banished men from the dance . . . he has crushed all his imitators beneath the weight of his glory." And Théophile Gautier, the poet-critic who wrote the libretto for *Giselle*, commented about the place of Perrot in the "species of monstrosity" (as he described the male dancer) as the one who "has vanquished our prejudices."

Gautier and other critics agreed that Perrot was "extremely ugly" and that from the waist up "he had the proportions of a tenor." But all agreed that his legs were superb and that his elevation, his lightness made him a "male Taglioni." Perrot did indeed dance with Taglioni and so successfully that the great ballerina, though young, ascendant, and popular, was jealous of his success. When, in one performance, he received greater applause and louder "bravos" than she, Taglioni not only refused to dance with him again but caused his dismissal from the Opéra.

Perrot, born in Lyon in 1810, was brought up in and around a theater where his father was a stage technician. He studied ballet from a local teacher and avidly watched all the dancers, acrobats, and mimes who came to Lyon. While still a child, he danced clown roles and monkey roles

(Jocko, the monkey, was a favorite character at the time) and observed the monkeys in the zoo. At thirteen he made his way to Paris and began studies with Auguste Vestris, who disagreed with others that Perrot was too small and too ugly to have a career as a classical dancer and guided him to his triumphs. It is said, however, that Vestris urged his pupil to keep moving on stage so that the audience would not have an opportunity to observe how homely he was and to stay in air as much as possible in order to conceal his shortness. Apparently, Perrot obeyed, for he was soon dubbed "Perrot l'aérien" and seemed to transform himself into the embodiment of a zephyr in that popular ballet, *Flore et Zéphyr*, especially revived for him and Taglioni shortly after he was engaged by the Opéra in Paris in 1830.

Also in 1830, Perrot made his London debut and became an instant favorite with English audiences, who continued to applaud him both as dancer and choreographer for years afterward.

The public in Italy and Austria were equally impressed with this lone *danseur* whom Gautier was soon to describe as the greatest dancer of his time. While performing in Naples, he met and fell in love with a fourteen-year-old girl who became his student, his mistress, his wife, and his superstar product. Her name was Carlotta Grisi and she was to be the first *Giselle*, the model and the inspiration of all the Giselles to follow around the world in the century-plus to follow.

Perrot, it is believed, wanted to choreograph *Giselle*, but because he had been dismissed from the Opéra the assignment went to Jean Coralli, principal choreographer at the Paris Opéra and one of the major choreographers of that period.

Print of Carlotta Grisi, the first Giselle, with her husband, Jules Perrot, who did not dance the first performance with her as Albrecht, but danced a later one.

But although Perrot's name does not appear on the program for the premiere in 1841, ballet historians believe that Perrot created all of Grisi's dances and mime scenes. The first Albrecht was Lucien Petipa, an excellent dancer and a gifted choreographer whose creative skills were obscured in history by the triumphs of his brother, Marius Petipa, one of the great choreographers of all time, the man who brought Russian ballet to its peak with *The Sleeping Beauty, Swan Lake* (for which his assistant, Lev Ivanov, did Acts II and IV), *La Bayadère, Don Quixote*, and other nineteenth-century classics. But Perrot did dance with Grisi in *Giselle* in London.

Perrot was not only the greatest and most successful male dancer of his era but also a choreographer of distinction, and his choreography was not only at the service of Grisi and the other great ballerinas of the Romantic Age but it also exalted them. For Perrot created ballets other than individual dances in *Giselle* for Grisi; he gave Fanny Cerrito one of her most famous dances, *Pas de Fascination*, and one of her greatest ballets, *Ondine*; for Fanny Elssler, he created *Faust* and restaged his *Esmeralda* (first danced by Grisi); for Denmark's Lucile Grahn, he choreographed one of her most successful ballets, *Eoline*; for Adèle Dumilâtre (the first Myrtha, Queen of the Wilis, in *Giselle*), *L'Aurore* (in which she made her London debut). In his long life—he lived to be eighty-two—he was permitted to choreograph only one ballet for the Opéra in Paris (1849), although as a choreographer he was hailed as one of the best in London, Naples, Milan, Vienna, Munich, and especially in St. Petersburg, where he served as ballet master from 1851 to 1859 and where some of his ballets, revised by Marius Petipa and others, survive to this day.

Perhaps his most spectacular association with the ballerina of the Romantic Age actually involved four of the five (only Elssler was missing) ballerinas of the period—Taglioni, Grisi, Cerrito, Grahn—in the historic *Pas de Quatre*, arranged for a command performance for Queen Victoria in 1845 (he had created a *pas de deux* for Elssler and Cerrito in 1843 by command of the Queen). Somehow, but not until several bursts of temper-

ament had nearly forced the cancellation of the event, he managed to get the four to dance together, to choreograph solos for each that exploited the specialties of each, and to put the dances in sequence so that no one was offended. To achieve the latter feat, he used female vanity as his weapon, for when each demanded precedence, and an impasse had been reached, he simply announced that the "eldest" would have that honor. Suddenly all of them were very young and retiring. Taglioni, who truly had seniority, got the place of honor.

Pas de Quatre, a *pièce d'occasion*, did not enter any repertory, although Anton Dolin, in the 1940s, met an old vaudeville dancer who informed him that her mother and three other variety dancers had learned it a century before and had performed it for many years in provincial vaudeville houses in England. Dolin himself, from studies of lithographs of the day, descriptions of the steps in reports published at the time, and a reading knowledge of the specialty of each ballerina, reconstructed this *Pas de Quatre* (1941) to the original Cesare Pugni score.

In an age that could bring such a generally accepted comment as "nothing is less graceful than a man who dances" and, in the words of Gautier, "there is nothing we like so little as to see male dancers," Jules Perrot "vanquished our prejudices" (also in the words of Gautier) to become the only male dancing star in one hundred years to match both the status and the artistry of the ballerina.

Lucien Petipa, the first Albrecht, possessed all the surface advantages that Perrot lacked. He was tall and exceedingly handsome and, because of his height, an ideal cavalier for the ballerina. In an age which despised the male dancer, he managed, like Perrot, to garner essential support, earning and retaining his fame and popularity not so much through the brilliance of his own dancing as through his great gifts as a partner, as a true *danseur noble*, the gentleman, the cavalier. Grisi, whose marriage to Perrot lasted barely seven years, was almost always paired with Petipa and they became lovers as well. As partners, they created leading roles in several major ballets, not only *Giselle* but also *La Péri, Le Diable à Quatre*,

Lucien Petipa, who danced the role of Albrecht the first time with Carlotta Grisi.

and *Paquita* among them.

Lucien, trained in childhood by his and Marius' father, Jean Petipa, outshone his brother both as a dancer and as a choreographer early in their careers, but by the end of the century, Lucien was all but forgotten and Marius, with almost half a century of power as ballet master and principal choreographer of the Russian Imperial Ballet, had become a dance immortal.

Arthur Saint-Léon, born Charles Michel in Paris, made his debut at thirteen in Munich (his father was ballet master in Stuttgart), but he made this debut in the dual capacity of dancer and violinist! As a pupil of the great violin virtuoso Paganini, Saint-Léon excelled as a violinist even though he elected to follow a career in dancing. He was able, however, to choreograph roles for himself which gave him opportunities to play the violin as well as dance on the ballet stage. A little more than a century after his double debut (1834), Maria Tallchief, undecided between a ca-

reer as a concert pianist and a dancer, made her debut in Los Angeles in a program half of which she played on the piano and the other half which she danced.

Saint-Léon wisely associated himself with a young ballerina on the threshold of fame, Fanny Cerrito. The two fell in love and after Saint-Léon had renounced his Jewish faith and been converted to Christianity, the Italian ballerina, a devout Roman Catholic, and her partner were married. Cerrito, even in ballets choreographed by such experts as Perrot, had displayed choreographic skill, the first female choreographer of significance since Sallé, but later Saint-Léon took on the choreographic assignments and created brilliantly for his wife.

Cerrito was showered with applause and flowers and caskets of jewels but Saint-Léon managed to win plaudits for himself: "Saint-Léon astonished everyone with the fearless vigor of his dancing and the ease with which he rose in the air; he knew how to win applause, which is not easy at a time when male dancing is out of favor." This was in 1847. Subsequently, Gautier wrote after attending the first Paris performance of the dancer-choreographer's *La Vivandière:* "Saint-Léon was also well received, which reminds us that not for a long time has a genuine male dancer been seen in France . . . Since Perrot's retirement, Saint-Léon is the only one [male] who has dared to dance at the Opéra for the sake of dancing, and all have been surprised by his success."

If the name Arthur Saint-Léon means anything at all to audiences of today, it is as choreographer of the durable and greatly beloved comedy-ballet *Coppélia,* which he created in 1870.

Late in the century came a brilliant young Italian dancer whose name is almost exclusively associated with teaching rather than with performing. Yet Enrico Cecchetti, born in Milan in 1850, became a prodigious virtuoso. Like Vestris the younger, he could whip off eight *pirouettes,* but to this turning feat, he added—and he was presumably the first—thirty-two *tours à la seconde,* the male's answer to the ballerina's famous thirty-two *fouettés,* first done by Pierina Legnani in *Cinderella* and later in the "Black Swan" se-

Perrot, by himself.

quence in *Swan Lake*. He was as accomplished an actor, or mime, as he was a virtuoso, and at the premiere of *The Sleeping Beauty* at the Maryinsky in 1890 he danced the Bluebird in the famous last act *pas de deux*, a showpiece for the *danseur*, and acted the role of the evil fairy, Carabosse.

But Cecchetti earned his lasting fame as a ballet master, teacher, coach, and the originator of a method of ballet instruction which bears his name and which is used by dancers and teachers throughout the world. It began, principally, in 1887 when Cecchetti headed a company of Italian dancers for appearances in St. Petersburg at the Arcadia Theater. The Russians were astounded by the advanced technique of the Italian visitors. The director of the Maryinsky and Petipa himself were impressed to the point of en-

gaging Cecchetti immediately, first as a dancer and, in 1888, as assistant ballet master. During his years with the Imperial Theater, he numbered among his pupils Kschessinska, Preobrajenska, and Egorova, three of the major ballerinas of the day and, after the Russian Revolution, the three most influential Russian teachers in Paris; Vaganova, who subsequently became the principal teacher at the Maryinsky; Trefilova, Karsavina, Nijinsky, and, especially, Anna Pavlova. In later years he became Pavlova's exclusive coach. From 1910 to 1919, when he opened his own school in London, Cecchetti was the principal teacher for Serge Diaghilev's Ballets Russes, which had come out of Russia to Paris and, later, to the rest of the world, to launch a new ballet era. To the great stars he had taught in Russia, he added as his pupils Massine, Lifar and Dolin, Markova, and countless others.

To these generations of ballet artists he brought not only the strict Italian school of instruction and his own very special genius as a teacher but also a teaching heritage that went in unbroken line back to the origins of professional ballet: Beauchamps (the first ballet master for Louis XIV), Pécourt, Dupré, Noverre, Gaetan Vestris, Dauberval, the masters of the seventeenth and eighteenth centuries; Vigano, Blasis, Lepri, Cecchetti of the nineteenth. Another royal branch from Gaetan to Auguste Vestris to Denmark's great Bournonville, sweeping from France to Denmark, and from Bournonville to Johansson (thence to Russia) who became a principal teacher at the Maryinsky, numbering Vaganova among his most important pupils, brought together in the Russian school, the direct lines of descent of the Royal House of Dance.

And it was Enrico Cecchetti who helped bring to an end a century of disrepute, of neglect, of contempt for the male dancer. He accomplished this not because he was a splendid dancer himself but because he was a master teacher, because he guided the male dance potential so skillfully that with the Diaghilev Era from 1909 to 1929 the male dancer could commence the difficult, tortuous climb back to equality with the ballerina. The first to achieve such eminence in this century was Vaslav Nijinsky.

4

THE MALE DANCER: AN AMERICAN HANG-UP

EQUAL RIGHTS for male dancers in America have not been fully realized even as the twentieth century draws to its close. One may ask, "Why?" While the royal and state theaters of Europe were auditioning little boys of seven and eight right along with little girls for enrollment in their national ballet schools, little American boys were rarely permitted to take ballet lessons and if they did they were jeered at. The successful boys attending the government-run ballet schools of Europe not only received a free education in academics and ballet and its related arts but also became members of the national companies, salaried for all of their lives and retired on pensions. In America, the rare male ballet student paid for his lessons, prayed for a job upon completion of his basic training (knowing he would pay for continuing ballet classes the rest of his life), settled for minimum pay, and faced late years with no security at all. Yet some sturdy American males accepted the challenge.

But why did this state of affairs exist? American Indians, especially males, were (and are) dancers, but with dance as an integral part of life and religion, not a profession. The newcomers to America—settlers and adventurers—had little time for the arts in a new and dangerous world.

(Overleaf) George Washington Smith, mid-nineteenth-century dancer. Smith was the only American male dancer in the nineteenth century to make a mark in classical ballet.

In the north particularly, the brand of spare, stark, and anti-ceremonial religion in power made theater of any sort, if not actually a sin, little better than self-indulgent frippery. The south, colonized with a greater percentage of aristocrats, found theater, balls, and fêtes most agreeable.

But with the end of the American Revolution and the founding of the Republic, anything that echoed of royal courts was anathema, and ballet, with its graces and echoes of courtly etiquette, seemed alien to the rough new world. For classical ballet then and now is firmly rooted in the elegance of the courtier—the sweeping *port de bras*, culminating in the grand *révérence* (a bow to Louis XIV and to majesty in general), is the child of etiquette—and the American pioneer, wearing buckskin and with rifle at the ready, probably never realized that the suave courtier, with lace-framed wrists, once exchanged handkerchief for sword to do battle for king and country.

The climate for ballet in a young republic was not hospitable. Perhaps if the technique had been that of the yet-to-be-invented modern dance of the twentieth century—a technique rooted in the natural movements of man, a spare and often stark style of dancing—the art of dance would have been grudgingly accepted by pioneers, and men dancers along with it. But that is an "iffy" comment, for until the middle of the twentieth century, none of the arts received government funding simply because to the average taxpayer the arts were a luxury. Not until the second half of the twentieth century did the average citizen and his representatives in municipal, state, and federal offices begin to suspect that in the arts they might well find both a national and a natural resource, and that of these arts, dance was bursting into a golden age of accomplishment, popularity, and (status!) recognition as a profit-making (in theory) business.

Another broadside striking the American male ballet dancer during the 1800s was the same lethal shot fired at the *danseur* abroad. With the rise, quite literally, of the ballerina onto *pointe*, the male was viewed as a lower species, the butt of derogatory comments, beneath contempt. In Europe, as we have seen, a handful of male dancers managed to achieve some recognition

John Durang, the first American dancer of note.

during the Age of Romantic Ballet and fitfully during the barren (except for Russia) closing decades of the last century. America had only one *premier danseur* of any distinction whatsoever during the entire nineteenth century, and before that a solitary male dancer, with admittedly elementary ballet qualifications, during the first three decades of the new nation. The *danseur* was George Washington Smith (circa 1820–99) and America's first professional dancer of distinction, John Durang (1768–1822).

Durang was probably not much of a ballet dancer by today's standards, or even by the ballet standards of the day in Europe, but he came along at a most propitious time: the American Revolution was ended, patriotism ran high, English performers were not welcome, the French Revolution had not yet taken place and the influx of French dancers had not begun, and Durang was an American whose immigrant father (from Strasbourg in Alsace-Lorraine) had fought in the American Revolution. Besides, John Durang was personable, a good dancer and versatile (actor, acrobat, juggler, writer, stage director, manager and . . . *danseur*).

Very probably he was self-taught, learning by watching other performers. He was born in York, Pennsylvania, but Philadelphia became his home base and Philadelphia was a city of culture. Indeed, it might be noted here and now that throughout the history of ballet in America, Philadelphia has been the producer of major dancers. Durang, America's first dancer of note, was a Philadelphian; the only nineteenth-century male dancer of any consequence, George Washington Smith, was a Philadelphian; America's first two ballerinas, Mary Ann Lee (the first American Giselle) and Augusta Maywood (the first American to star at the Opéra in Paris), were both Philadelphians; Catherine Littlefield, ballerina, the first to produce the full-length *The Sleeping Beauty* in America and to take an American ballet troupe to Europe (her own Littlefield Ballet) was a Philadelphian, as was her dancing sister, Dorothie; Karen Conrad, a Littlefield pupil, and a star of the American Ballet Theatre in its first years, was a Philadelphian, and on and on to this day.

Durang made his debut in 1784 when he was seventeen years old. The Continental Congress, before and during the Revolution, had frowned on theatrical enterprises and during certain periods plays and dances and any form of entertainments were banned by law. To get around the law, producers presented "lectures" and patriotic pageants. Durang's first employer was an Englishman, Lewis Hallam, who had been a successful actor in America for many years before the Revolution and whose father was both an actor and a manager. Lewis Hallam was probably the first to return to the onetime colonies after the war and because of his family's renown and his own popularity he had little trouble in assembling a company and obtaining a theater (the old Southwark), but he could not get a license to present entertainments, hence the "lectures."

John Durang may possibly have studied dancing briefly from an Italian ballet master who passed swiftly through Philadelphia, but it is likely that he did not receive any thorough ballet instruction until the French influx of dancers several years later. But dance he did in character dances and in all manner of patriotic spectacles and in such Americanized versions of *commedia dell'arte* as *Harlequin in Philadelphia*. In New York City, which had suffered under British occupation troops, English performers were booed but young Durang was cheered. So it is difficult to say how much of his early success was due to talent and how much to his fortunate nationality.

Talent he must have had, for his career was a long one. As he went along, he became more directly involved in ballet. In 1792, Alexander Placide, a French ballet dancer who also performed on wire, did circus acts, and played the violin, arrived in America with his wife and played Philadelphia and, especially, Charleston. Durang worked with him briefly in the Old American Company and learned from him. Subsequently, Durang performed an Indian dance in what was probably the first American opera, *Tammany*, and danced in the first true ballet, *La Forêt Noire*, in which the star was Madame Gardie, born in Santo Domingo but the first dancer to be received as a star, a prima ballerina, in America. Durang appeared with her, usually in small parts, in ballets created for her by a Frenchman, Francisquy, associated with Placide in Charleston, and later a choreographer for the Old American Company. The ballets he created for that company made it possible for a ballet troupe to come into being within the framework of the bigger theatrical enterprise. This was John Durang's major training ground as a ballet dancer. In later years, as a producer himself, Durang presented many ballets and pageants which had their roots, or their models, in Francisquy ballets.

But of all his dances, a hornpipe, which became universally known as *Durang's Hornpipe*, was his trademark. He danced it throughout his career. Its guises changed, of course, and once, to add variety, he performed it while blindfolded on a stage littered with thirteen eggs, not cracking one! His son has left a detailed description of the hornpipe, the music exists, and the man himself, in his old age, drew sketches of himself in his hornpipe costume (as well as in costumes for other roles). The mixture of terminology in describing the steps of the *Durang's Hornpipe* provides us with some clues. The first step is a *glissade* round; later you find whirligig with beats down immediately followed by *sissonne* and *entrechats* back, a *terre-à-terre* instruction leading into a jockey crotch down!

John Durang, his sister, his wife, and his children were all dancers, and actors, too, of course. He danced more than once for George Washington since the First President was not only a theatergoer but a great believer in dancing as a symbol of culture and graciousness and as a discipline in behavior. General and Mrs. Washington presided over social dance events, but dance in the theater was to be savored also.

Our first American dancer performed in plays, pageants, and ballets too numerous to mention but his place in our history may well be characterized by a production of the Old American Company in 1790 in New York, *The Independence of America*, or *The Ever Memorable Fourth of July, 1776*, a pantomime with Mme. Gardie as the spirit of America, as the Declaration of Independence was read. The role of First Citizen was played, appropriately, by John Durang.

John Durang died in 1822. Ten years later, a stonecutter named George Washington Smith made his bow in his native Philadelphia as "a clog, hornpipe, and flatfoot dancer." It was not until Fanny Elssler came to America in 1841 for what turned out to be a two-year tour that Smith had any real opportunity to study ballet. His chance came when the great Viennese star arrived in Philadelphia and needed "pick-up" dancers to support her in ballets. This was not an uncommon practice in Elssler's case, for she could not travel with a full troupe at all times yet she often appeared in full-length ballets such as *La Sylphide* (the Taglioni favorite) or *La Gypsy*, *La Tarentule*, and other earthy ballets more suited to her style. It was the responsibility of her ballet master, Louis Sylvain (born Sullivan), to recruit possible dancers in the cities on tour and train them for ensemble work in the ballets. This

must have been a forbidding task in days when few girls and almost no men had any training in ballet. For men, Sylvain had to pick the hoofers, the acrobats, the actors, the mimes. George Washington Smith was among the lucky ones. It changed his life.

Sylvain was Elssler's partner and he coached Smith well. The young American studied avidly with him. Sylvain was not only an accomplished ballet dancer, he was also a master of the English pantomime (his brother, Barry Sullivan, was a prominent actor in England) and taught his Philadelphian pupil all of the steps, postures, gestures associated with the role of Harlequin. Harlequinades were still popular in America and would remain so for years to come. Smith became the definitive American Harlequin of the century and passed on his knowledge of Harlequin's attitudes and of early eighteenth-century ballet to his youngest son (he had eleven children), Joseph, who was to become a dancer and a Broadway choreographer through the 1920s.

When Sylvain departed for Europe before the end of the Elssler tour, the ballerina had to find another partner. A Frenchman was one but it is almost certain that George Washington Smith was another. As an elderly man, he reminisced about her in a press interview and told of how Sylvain was his major teacher and how he and the ballerina were on friendly terms to the degree that she gave him a valuable present on her departure for Europe. But what roles he actually danced with her remain obscure. His son Joseph assures us in his writing that his father did indeed partner "The Divine Fanny."

After Elssler's departure, Smith was through with stonecutting, with clog and flatfoot dancing. He was a *danseur*. He treasured her parting gift, an engraved gold pencil, and he named one of his daughters after her, Fanny Elssler Smith. He probably began intensive studies with P. H. Hazard, a Philadelphia ballet instructor, formerly with the Opéra in Paris. Hazard was the teacher of the two Philadelphia girls, Mary Ann Lee and Augusta Maywood, America's first ballerinas.

In 1842, with the Elssler troupe gone, Smith made use of his Harlequinade training and appeared in a pantomime called *Mazulme, or The*

Black Raven of the Tombs. This proved to be a popular success and it became a staple in Smith's repertory for the next twenty years. Smith performed in pantomimes, opera ballets and in all manner of theatrical presentations while he continued his studies with local ballet masters, such as Hazard, and visiting choreographers. In 1845 he joined forces with Mary Ann Lee, who had just returned from a period of study at the Opéra in Paris (it is possible that Smith was studying in Paris at the same time). On January 1, 1845, the first American production of *Giselle* was presented in Boston with Mary Ann Lee, who had staged it, as Giselle and George Washington Smith as the first American Albrecht. He and Mary Ann Lee performed together in *Giselle, La Fille du Danube*, and other ballets for two years. Critics in those days always dwelt on the artistry, personality, accomplishments of the ballerina, and the *danseur* was mentioned only in passing, if at all. Critics, however, did take some note of Smith, perhaps out of patriotism because he was American, and referred to his "*tours de force.*" Smith and Lee toured extensively, traveling as far as New Orleans.

When Mary Ann Lee retired because of illness (she made a brief comeback a few seasons later), Smith became the partner of the third ballerina of note in early American ballet, Julia Turnbull, who had danced with Elssler on her American tour. With Turnbull he appeared in *Nathalie, ou La Latière Suisse* (an Elssler favorite), and as Albrecht to Turnbull's Giselle. These and other ballets were supervised by Smith, who had become principal dancer and ballet master of the Bowery Theater in New York in 1847. Late in 1848, Giovanna Ciocca, an Italian ballerina and a pupil of Blasis, arrived in America and Smith eventually served her as a partner. Later came Louise Ducy-Barre from Paris and Smith partnered her also. His most notorious associate was Lola Montez, a beautiful woman and an expert lover (she numbered the King of Bavaria among her conquests) but a limited dancer. For Montez, Smith turned choreographer and created for her full-length ballets as well as scenes and dances that would show her off to her best advantage while concealing her technical limitations. Smith

must have done well, for although the critics knew that she was not of ballerina stature, they were appreciative of her performing. But in the long run, Smith as choreographer for Lola was more successful than Lola as a ballerina, so she soon left that phase of her career behind her.

In 1859, Smith joined a troupe from Milan, the Ronzani Ballet, which numbered among its youngest members the child of one of the dancing couples. His name was Enrico Cecchetti. Smith danced successfully with the Ronzanis. He was approximately forty years old and at the peak of his career. A decade later he revived *Giselle*—although interest in the romantic ballets of decades before had passed—and danced Albrecht for the last time. But his career continued for many more years as dancer, pantomimist, ballet master, and choreographer. His son Joseph, born in 1875, was the only one of the children to enter the theater and he learned all he could from his father until America's first *premier danseur*, G. W. Smith, died in 1899.

Today, we are so proud of our virtuosi, of Nureyev, Baryshnikov, and Bujones, of the dazzling contenders for the laurel wreaths such as Dupond from France and the young dancing athletes from Japan or Hungary or Belgium who display their prowess at the great ballet competitions in Varna, Moscow, Tokyo. So how did America's one and only *premier danseur* of the last century rate in terms of technical skill?

Lillian Moore's researches came up with the information that when Smith studied Harlequin with Sylvain, *entrechats, tours en l'air*, and *pirouettes à la seconde* were to be expected of the interpreter. If we are to believe Joseph Smith's descriptions of his father, from whom he studied (and he too became a virtuoso in ballet but in an era when ballet was of little interest and show business dancing of more moment), George Washington Smith was capable of *entrechat-huit*, triple *tours en l'air*, and as many as 120 uninterrupted *pirouettes à la seconde*. George Washington Smith, onetime stonecutter and flatfoot dancer, with his funny pantaloons and bristling mustaches, was no one to be ashamed of. He was all we had in the entire nineteenth century and he did us proud!

5

NIJINSKY: THE CLOWN OF GOD

MAURICE BÉJART, founder-director of Belgium's national ballet, the Ballet of the 20th Century, created a full-length, spectacular fantasy-biography called *Nijinsky, Clown of God*. This 1971 creation contains echoes in movement of historical ballets with which Nijinsky was associated—*Le Spectre de la Rose, Scheherazade,* and especially *Petrouchka* with its puppet-clown—and visions of dances Nijinsky performed with a giant cross during his own madness. The English playwright Richard Crane in 1975 saw the first production of *Clownmaker*, his play in two acts and twenty-five scenes, also a fantasy-biography. In 1918, as he embarked on his voyage into madness, Nijinsky wrote a diary. In one passage, he says, "People like an odd and peculiar man and they will leave me alone, calling me a 'mad clown.'"

Also in his diary, he wrote: "I like simple people but not stupidity, because I see no feeling in that. Intelligence stops people from developing. I feel God and God feels me." He signed his diary at its close, "God and Nijinsky, Saint Moritz-Dorf, Villa Guardamunt, February 27, 1919." In his diary, he called himself "a clown of God"; the world called him *Le Dieu de la Danse*.

Vaslav Nijinsky was born in Kiev in 1888 of Polish parents who were dancers. He attended the Imperial Ballet School in St. Petersburg, where he excelled as a dancer but stumbled miserably in his academic studies. The late Anatole Bourman, a classmate of Nijinsky's and a continuing friend, felt that his remarkable dancing

(Overleaf) Nijinsky as the favorite slave in *Scheherazade*.

gifts were apparent from the start, so much so that other boys in the class were jealous of him. Bourman in his book *The Tragedy of Nijinsky* writes of these early days with more knowledge than anyone else and with a classmate's nonpoeticized comments; Tamara Karsavina, who was to become his most celebrated partner in the days of the Diaghilev Ballets Russes, recalled his remarkable elevation and, in her superb book, *Theatre Street*, provides us with a close picture of Nijinsky the young artist; his wife, Romola, in her one-view, understandably slanted book about him, *Nijinsky*, gives us an intimate portrait; and Lincoln Kirstein, in his monumental, gloriously illustrated *Nijinsky Dancing* provides dance lovers of today with a scholarly yet wonderfully vivid view of the great dancer.

There are thousands of written words about Nijinsky; a fair selection (though not nearly enough) of photographs of him; only fragments of movie film. His career, from his graduation from the Imperial School in St. Petersburg in 1908 until his last, half-mad performance in 1919, was far shorter than that of other great male dancers who had made, or were to make, dance history. In fact, his fame rests on the years 1909, when he first danced outside of Russia in Diaghilev's debut season in Paris, to 1916, when he retired to Switzerland to live through the remainder of World War I. Yet in those seven years he created a legend, for the very name "Nijinsky" remains magical. He was the greatest male dancer of his day; perhaps he is the greatest male dancer of the twentieth century; possibly, the greatest male ballet dancer of all time. For ballet in this century, there are two lasting models, two deities whose names alone identify them to the world: Anna Pavlova, Vaslav Nijinsky.

The genius of Nijinsky was not exclusively physical, although this was considered sensational by audiences and critics. He could execute *entrechat-huit* easily and *entrechat-dix* if asked to do so. The *pirouettes* were multiple. The *batterie* electrifying. The body could move from the noble lines, gently curved, of classical ballet to the almost two-dimensional angularities he devised for himself and his associates in his own *L'Après-midi d'un Faune*. But his elevation was

viewed as phenomenal; he vaulted high in soaring arcs of flight, unlike the "split" leaps introduced to the West by Bolshoi Ballet dancers in the 1950s and 1960s; he had *ballon* as well as altitude so that the spring into the air and the breathless pause there seemed to transform space into his natural home. When asked about his ability to seemingly suspend a movement in space, he replied, according to Karsavina: "No! No! Not difficult. You just have to go up and then pause a little up there."

Physically, he was short with almost overly muscular legs and rather heavy ankles. The thighs were also large and the waist was not small. All of these characteristics can be studied in the photographs of Nijinsky. Those who had seen him offstage reported that in a room full of celebrities he would be overlooked, because, aside from the Oriental cast to his face, he seemed quite ordinary. Since he was retiring, not talkative, and conservative in street dress, he could go unnoticed.

Yet on stage he was transformed. The big muscles propelled him with lightness into space; they enabled him to move with incredible speed across the stage. They did not weigh him, they freed him. The cast of the face became exotic, mysterious, ranging from the noble mien of Albrecht in *Giselle*, through the sensual head posture of the Faun, to the near-mad hero in his last ballet, *Tyl Eulenspiegel*. That he was also a superb actor is a fact. Each role was conceived, experienced, shaped, projected, and, I dare say, lived by Nijinsky. The great actress Sarah Bernhardt is said to have exclaimed: "I'm afraid! I'm afraid! Here is the greatest actor in the world!"

Carl Van Vechten, the critic and author and just about the only knowledgeable voice for dance in America before the 1920s, reviewed Diaghilev's Ballets Russes for the New York *Times*. And in 1916 he wrote: "And how few of us can view the art of Nijinsky without emotion!" Earlier, Van Vechten had seen Nijinsky, and for the first time, in Paris. Then he wrote: "Nijinsky completely effaced the memory of all the male dancers I had previously seen." When Van Vechten saw him again, this time in America, in 1916, the dancer had spent two years interned in Hungary during World War I. Van Vechten, before the performance, was worried: "I can say for myself that I was probably a good deal more nervous than Nijinsky on the occasion of his first appearance in America. It would have been a cruel disappointment to me to discover that his art had deteriorated during the intervening years since I had last seen him. My fears were soon dissipated. A few seconds after he, as the Rose Ghost, had bounded through the window, it was evident that he was in possession of all his powers; nay, more, that he had added to the refinement and polish of his style. I had called Nijinsky's dancing perfection in years gone by, because it far surpassed that of his nearest rival; now he had surpassed himself."

Nijinsky, still in his twenties when he danced for the last time, became a legend in his own time and for a later day also. But in this instance, legend was fact. He was the greatest dancer, perhaps the greatest actor too, in the world. His last major tour was in 1916; his last performance,

when he was half-mad, was in 1919 in a hotel in Switzerland; his body died in 1950. Perhaps both the dancing career and the madness were predictable; the genius was not. He had been born in Kiev, not because it was home, but because his dancing parents were on tour. The family had been dancers, acrobats, circus performers for generations. Dancing was in the blood. There was madness too. His father was irresponsible, given to strange behavior. His brother was ultimately institutionalized. Vaslav himself was withdrawn, moody, a hopeless student, an innocent who was an easy prey to fawning, to pressures, to the machinations of those who were jealous of his dancing genius.

His mother, not wishing an itinerant life for this son, enrolled him in the Imperial School of Ballet at St. Petersburg in 1899 (some historians give the date as 1898 and others 1900); in 1907 he graduated and his performance in a series of ballet excerpts was so brilliant that Mathilde Kschessinska, the *prima ballerina assoluta* and all-powerful friend of the Tsar, invited the young boy to partner her in special performances at the Summer Palace; teachers, critics, colleagues, and public were equally impressed and Nijinsky, although listed as *corps de ballet*, began his career as a soloist-principal.

It was important, too, that Vaslav Nijinsky, with his superior talent, should emerge at the time he did. Ballet was about to be reborn. In Western Europe it was almost dead; only artists such as Carlotta Zambelli and Albert Aveline gave any distinction to ballet in Paris, and in Russia the Age of Petipa was grinding to a halt. Serge Diaghilev, not a creative artist but a creator of artists, was launched with the then avant-garde in literature, painting, music, and, through Michel Fokine, ballet. Fokine was in revolt against the strictures of classical ballet, against the format that Petipa had devised and which had served him so brilliantly. The conservatives in authority held Fokine back and his early creations were often performed outside the repertory of the Imperial Ballet or his projects were totally rejected. Nijinsky excelled in the classics, bringing new life, new meaning to such old works as *Giselle*, but his dancing also stirred Fokine's in-

terest and it conquered Diaghilev wholly.

When Diaghilev took his Ballets Russes to Paris in 1909—the year before he had produced an enormously successful season of Russian opera in Paris—the Russian dancers, the Fokine ballets, the decor of Bakst and Benois and Roerich, music and staging took Paris by storm. And Nijinsky became the center of the furor. Most of the dancers were under contract to the Imperial Theater, Nijinsky among them, and were free to dance Diaghilev seasons only when at liberty. But Diaghilev had no intention of permitting his company to be only a seasonal one. There was no place at the Imperial Theater for Fokine to experiment. He cast his lot with Diaghilev. In 1911, Nijinsky became free—he was fired by the Imperial Theater—to join Diaghilev. He was dismissed for wearing a costume, or lack of it, displeasing to the Dowager Empress. By today's standards, his final costume was indeed standard. The ballet was *Giselle* and he wore tights. BUT, he did not wear the little pair of trunks over them that were prescribed apparel for the males. Even the Bolshoi Ballet when it first came to Western Europe and America in the 1950s required its male dancers to wear these little boxing trunks or long tunics or underpants (rather than a dance belt) beneath the tights. So Nijinsky was fired. Some historians hold to the opinion that Diaghilev put him up to it just so that he would be dismissed and become free to join the Ballets Russes.

Diaghilev was Nijinsky's employer, his mentor, his lover, and most of all his protector in all matters personal and professional. All Nijinsky needed to think about was his own dancing and, soon, his own choreography. From the start, he was a phenomenon in the West and the ballets in which he captured critics and audiences everywhere included a diversity of technical and dramatic, musical and stylistic challenges and opportunities. They were: *Giselle*, the enduring ballet of the Romantic Age; *Les Sylphides*, Fokine's evocation of that Romantic Age as represented by Taglioni's *La Slyphide*; Fokine's *Pavillon d'Armide* (1907), which he first danced with Pavlova, later with Kschessinska; *Cléopâtre*, the Fokine ballet first danced with Pavlova at the Maryinsky in St. Petersburg in 1908; and Fokine's *Le Car-*

Nijinsky with Tamara Karsavina
in *Le Spectre de la Rose.*

naval, in which he was Harlequin; *Scheherazade*, in the role of the sensual, savage Slave; *Le Spectre de la Rose*, as the evanescent spirit of the rose; *Petrouchka*, the title part of the puppet with a human soul; *Narcisse*, *Le Dieu Bleu*, *Daphnis and Chloe*. In addition to these Fokine ballets, Nijinsky starred in his own first choreographic effort, *L'Après-midi d'un Faune* (1912), an avant-garde work in which the movement style was derived from ancient bas-reliefs; the erotic ending, in which the Faun presses his body against the fallen scarf of a nymph in a simulated sex contact, caused a scandal in Paris and for years to come, with other interpreters, was censored. His *Jeux*, with sexual overtones, was contemporary and related a tennis match to a love match; his *Sacre du Printemps* caused a riot in Paris, but as much for the music of the young Igor Stravinsky (who fled the theater in terror) as for the primitive, feral choreography. His fourth and last ballet was *Tyl Eulenspiegel*, created in America in 1916, in which he starred as the legendary prankster.

Diaghilev's Ballets Russes made such an impact in Paris that almost in an instant it launched the renascence of ballet in Western Europe and elevated the art of dancing once again to a plane of equality with the other arts. The ignoble, despised male was restored too and instantly by the flashing virility and athletic prowess of Adolph Bolm, a *demi-caractère* dancer engaged for the Ballets Russes, in the Polovetsian Dances from *Prince Igor* and of Nijinsky, who was described as "miraculeux" and "the new Vestris." Still, it was the "today" and not the "yester-

day" which entranced the French press and public. Karsavina and Nijinsky were much admired and praised in *Giselle* but the style and especially the old Adolphe Adam score seemed old-fashioned, for the day had not yet arrived when great interpreters of the Romantic Age ballets would restore to contemporary dance repertories the masterpieces of the early nineteenth century, giving them new luster, new life, just as Maria Callas was to do for grand opera in the 1950s by leading the way to the restoration of Romantic Age operas to modern opera repertory. For the Parisians of 1909, the Fokine ballets, with new concepts of choreography, of decor, of music, of libretto were what they wanted. And Nijinsky was their favorite.

For his final performance, in 1919, just a decade after he had burst upon the world, Nijinsky danced for an invited audience of two hundred in a hotel room in Switzerland. In advance, he would not say what he would perform. When the time came, he spoke as well as performed a program of his own making. The final dance saw a roll of black cloth and a roll of white spread across the floor to mark a mighty cross. Nijinsky himself stood in the position of the Cross and announced to the audience that he would dance about the recent war with its sufferings, its destructions, and its deaths, a war he blamed on his audience. He terrified his wife and he terrified his public and he knew it: "My dances were frightening." Later he wrote: "I am beginning to understand God. I know that he creates movement, and so I ask Him to help . . ."

In Béjart's *Nijinsky, Clown of God*, the final dance is re-created—and superbly by Jorge Donn—with all the terror that witnesses to the original reported. Béjart conceived it on a vast scale, as a spectacle of the artist crucified. In the modest staging of the first American production of Richard Crane's *Clownmaker*, Nijinsky—superbly acted by Stephen Lang—cries out: "I can fly to the sun, touch it if I want . . . I have to stop in the clean air. I cannot come down now." Like Icarus of Greek myth, he flew too close to the sun, but unlike Icarus, Vaslav Nijinsky never fell from that perfection which astounded his contemporaries and made him a dance immortal.

6

FURTHER DIAGHILEV DISCOVERIES: MASSINE, LIFAR, DOLIN

F OLLOW that ACT? Murder!" In vaudeville, or in any kind of show business, great performers have great acts that are so sure-fire that no other artist wants to follow. For the newly re-established *danseur* in the first two decades of this century, Vaslav Nijinsky was an almost impossible act to follow. Yet someone had to. The producing genius of Diaghilev was not about to be aborted by the defection of a principal male dancer, no matter how irreplaceable he seemed. Diaghilev had made an international star of Nijinsky. He had given him more than exposure outside his native Russia. He had given him guidance, he had placed him in a new and vital repertory not to be found in St. Petersburg, he had advised him, educated him, disciplined him as well as loved him.

When he dismissed Nijinsky, because he had married without permission, in 1913—there was a brief re-association for touring purposes in 1916—Diaghilev went talent scouting for a successor. In Moscow, in 1913, he found young (eighteen years old) Leonide Massine and saw in him a possible—but entirely different in appearance and talent—successor to Nijinsky. He had begun to guide Nijinsky into a choreographic career while providing him with ever greater performing opportunities. He planned the same for Massine.

Lest it seem that Diaghilev had only a single male star with his Ballets Russes when Nijinsky reigned, it should be noted again that Adolph Bolm, from 1909 to 1914 (he even performed for Diaghilev in 1908 when the great impresario introduced Russian opera to Paris), was enormously popular with the public, particularly in character parts and most especially of all as the Chief Warrior in the Polovetsian Dances (by Fokine) from Borodin's opera *Prince Igor*. After Bolm left, there was Leon Woizikovsky, a brilliant character dancer, to take on the *Prince Igor* and similar assignments.

After Nijinsky, it seemed that those who followed were slightly less than great. Massine, as it turned out, was earmarked for fame as a choreographer, but as a dancer, especially as a character dancer and as one who would be enormously effective in new ballets (many created by himself) with strong modern dance elements, he would also win international fame. In 1914 he danced his first leading role for Diaghilev in Fokine's *Legend of Joseph*, thus replacing Nijinsky as the upcoming principal male dancer, and the following year, 1915, he created his first ballet, *Soleil de Nuit*, replacing Fokine (who re-

Massine in his own ballet, *Le Tricorne*.

Leonide Massine when he first joined
Diaghilev's Ballets Russes in the *Legend of Joseph*,
the first ballet in which he appeared.

Massine and the great ballerina Alexandra Danilova
in "The Blue Danube Waltz" from the Massine ballet
Le Beau Danube.
Fred Fehl

turned to Russia in 1914 at the outbreak of
World War I) as Diaghilev's principal choreographer.

Massine, throughout his long dancing career,
not only excelled as a character dancer, as an actor-dancer, and as an exponent of what might be
described as "free-style" dancing but also
achieved the undisputed status of star. Small and
lithe, he was also dynamic and his large black
eyes, wonderfully expressive of passion, arrogance,
mischief, and even spiritual ecstasy, could convey
their messages to the last row of the largest theaters.

Massine did indeed try his skills in a few of
Nijinsky's and other *danseurs'* roles, but he soon
became identified almost exclusively with parts
he created for himself in his own ballets. After
Fokine, Massine was certainly the most important choreographer to be developed by Diaghilev
and to retain a choreographic supremacy long
after Diaghilev died. But here, we are concerned
not so much with his choreographic achievements as with his own performing; since the two
are closely linked in many ballets, a look at his
ballets is essential.

Massine was a good Spanish dancer, not an
equal to a native Spaniard (such as Escudero or
the later Antonio) trained in dance, but accomplished in a somewhat balleticized Spanish dance
style. One of Massine's most popular ballets was
Le Tricorne (*The Three-Cornered Hat*), created
in 1919 to music of de Falla and decor and cos-

Mikhail Mordkin with Anna Pavlova in *The Pharaoh's Daughter*, a ballet from the days of the Russian Imperial Ballet.

tumes by Picasso. Tamara Karsavina, Diaghilev's prima ballerina and Nijinsky's most frequent partner, played the Miller's Wife to Massine's Miller. The great Spanish dancer, Argentinita, also danced the Wife on special occasions and it was she who was the inspiration for another of Massine's enormously popular Spanish-flavored ballets, *Capriccio Espagnol*.

In addition to his success in his Spanish-style ballets, Massine was adored by the international public in comedy parts, among them, a Can-Can Dancer in his *La Boutique Fantasque* and as the rich, gauche, girl-crazy Peruvian in one of the most popular ballets ever created, *Gaîté Parisienne*. Turning romantic, he was unforgettable as the dreaming, romantic Hussar in his own *Le Beau Danube*, another perennial favorite. In *Boutique*, *Danube*, and *Gaîté* the partner most fre-

quently associated with him was the great ballerina Alexandra Danilova, a junior ballerina with Diaghilev's Ballets Russes and the prima ballerina of the later Ballet Russe de Monte Carlo (which Massine directed from 1938 to 1945). The intensely religious side of Massine, manifesting itself most strongly during recent years, was most powerfully realized in 1938 when he produced to Hindemith's music, his *Saint Francis* (known in Europe as *Nobilissima Visione*), a ballet biography of the beloved Saint.

Elements of religion, myth, faith, and ethics are present in several of his historic "symphonic

Serge Lifar in George Balanchine's first major ballet, *Apollo* (then called *Apollon Musagète*).

44

La Chatte, with Lifar and group.

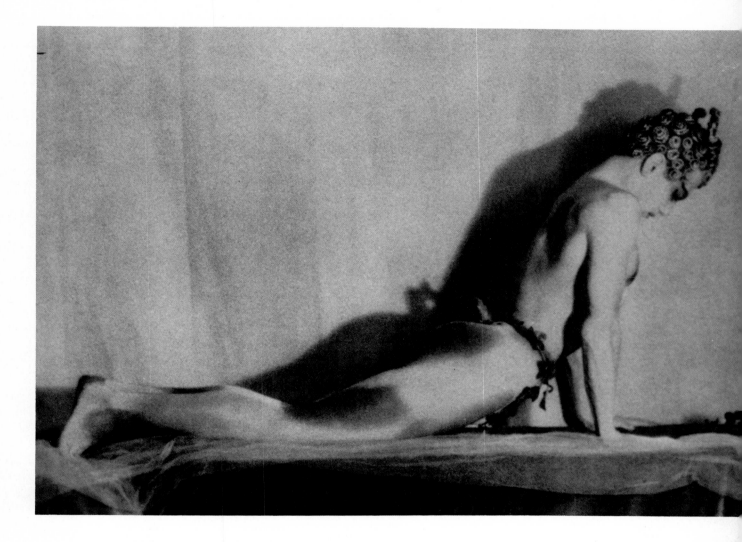

Lifar as the Faun in
Nijinsky's *Afternoon of a Faun.*

ballets," in which he introduced a wholly new musico-choreographic element into classical ballet. Isadora Duncan, Ruth St. Denis, Ted Shawn, and their modern dance disciples had long since believed they had the right to dance to already composed classical music if they so desired. (The ballet had almost exclusively employed scores especially composed for dancing.) It was daring of Massine, therefore, to take music of Tchaikovsky (symphonic music, not his ballet scores), Brahms, Berlioz, Shostakovich composed as symphonies and dance to them! The music world was shocked, outraged! Composers and critics railed in print and in debates against Massine's "des-

ecration" of great music. But the "symphonic ballets" became tremendously popular, the musical bigots were bested, and for some years Massine's *Les Présages*—Tchaikovsky (1933), *Choréartium*—Brahms (1933), *Symphonie Fantastique*—Berlioz (1936), and *Rouge et Noir*—Shostakovich (1939) were cornerstones of the Ballet Russe de Monte Carlo's repertory.

Fokine's ballets for Diaghilev had restored to

the male dancer much of his long-lost eminence. Fokine too was a dancer and a very good one. He was personable, stylish, versatile, and technically strong. With his wife, the team of Fokine and Fokina was popular not only in Europe but also in America, which was, starting in 1923, to become his headquarters until his death in 1942. But history turns to Fokine and his ballet reformation and to the ballet masterpieces he produced as one of the most influential choreographers of this century rather than to the dancer. John Masefield, England's poet laureate (appointed by His Majesty King George V in 1930), in dedicating his book *Tribute to Ballet* (1938) to Fokine designates him as "the ballet master" and says of him, "He seeks a beauty never sold in shops."

With Massine, the dancer was every bit as important as the choreographer in the minds of the public. Massine was the undisputed male star of the Ballets Russes de Monte Carlo when it was directed by Colonel Wassily de Basil in 1933. He himself assumed the direction of R. Blum's rival company, the Ballet Russe de Monte Carlo, in 1938. (The spelling was changed to the singular in 1935.)

Leonide Massine, dancer, may be considered one of the great dancers, not in the sense that Auguste Vestris or Nijinsky or today's Nureyev and Baryshnikov are regarded as virtuosi as well as sensitive artists, but, rather, as a nonvirtuosic dancer of distinctiveness and distinction in a new style of male dance roles in a new, exploring and developing age of ballet. In other words, he did not stress the physical technique of the ballet classroom but, rather, stressed expressivity of movement and gesture.

The last of Diaghilev's male dancer protégés was the Kiev-born Serge Lifar, brought to Paris by Bronislava Nijinska to join the Ballets Russes. The year was 1923 and Lifar was eighteen. Two years later he was made *premier danseur*. Diaghilev supervised his continuing studies with Nicholas Legat, the teacher who had taught Nijinsky, Bolm, Fokine, and other stellar male dancers at the Imperial School in St. Petersburg, and, of course, with Cecchetti and also Pierre Vladimiroff (who later became a principal teacher at

the School of American Ballet).

Lifar, the dancer, was considered by many of his contemporaries among critics and ballet-omanes as the most brilliant male dancer of his era. Before he himself turned to choreography, many important ballets were created especially for him. Nijinska, of course, cast him in her new *Les Fâcheux* and *Le Train Bleu* as early as 1924, and Massine featured him in both *Zéphire et Flore* and in *Les Matelots* (1925). The year after George Balanchine defected from Russia to the West (1924), Lifar was cast in Balanchine's first ballet for Diaghilev, *Barabau*. Subsequently Balanchine, who became choreographer for Diaghilev until the impresario's death in 1929, created two of his all-time masterpieces, *Apollo* (1928) and *The Prodigal Son* (1929), in which Lifar danced the title roles.

When he started with Diaghilev, Lifar was little better than an amateur. The technique was elementary. But the teenager was diligent and ambitious as well as exotic-looking and beautifully built. With remorseless application to study, he perfected a technique that allowed him to accomplish triple turns in air and supported him brilliantly as the Bluebird in *The Sleeping Beauty*, as Siegfried in *Swan Lake*, and as Albrecht in *Giselle*. His repertory later included Nijinsky's roles in *Le Spectre de la Rose* and *L'après-midi d'un Faune*. And, of course, he had no peers in those ballets built for his talents by Nijinska, Massine, Balanchine.

Diaghilev saw to it that his newest, youngest, and final dance protégé received thorough training in ballet and that he also received a unique education through exposure to the artistries and persons of the foremost painters, composers, librettists, poets, sophisticates of the day. When Diaghilev died, he left Lifar his priceless collection of designs, scores, and irreplaceable notes. Just before he died, he presided over Lifar's choreography for a new production of Stravinsky's *Renard*. The result was so promising that in Lifar, Diaghilev seemed to rediscover those gifts for performing and creating that he had lost with Nijinsky. Unfortunately, he did not live to see the fulfillment of his predictions.

Lifar did, indeed, go on to become the most

Anton Dolin in his days with Diaghilev.

influential dancer and choreographer and, ultimately, all-powerful ballet director in France. In 1930, a year after Diaghilev's death, he was appointed director of the historic Paris Opéra Ballet, a position he held until 1945, returning again in 1947 and remaining as ballet master and chief choreographer until 1959. During those decades, he was the *premier danseur étoile* and his ballets, representing a huge output, constituted the core of the repertory at the Opéra and gave French ballet its special cast and characteristics for thirty years.

Whatever non-French balletgoers may think of Lifar's creations—and they have not enjoyed much popularity outside of France—it is a fact that if Diaghilev's Ballets Russes shocked the French out of their balletic lethargy, a moribund condition that had lasted half a century, it is equally true that Lifar *did* something about a desiccated ballet tradition still concerned with fairy tales and productions that were huge but tasteless, big but without substance. The dancers were lazy, the girls overweight, the total standards far below those set by Diaghilev. Lifar brought not only a new repertory of his own devising, but also totally new principles of choreography, streamlined performers, challenging, adventuresome themes.

Of his many experimental ballets, his *Icare* was one of the most successful. It was a perfect vehicle for his own technical and dramatic skills and choreographically it led ballet into that area explored only by modern dancers and that was to let dance stand as independent of its sister arts and not as a slave to either the composer or the designer. Thus, he choreographed *Icare* without music, creating his own movement rhythms and phrases in purely dance terms. When it was complete, he commissioned a percussion sound-effects score to support a finished art product.

Lifar, tempestuous and controversial, represented by himself an entire era in the long history of French ballet. His influence was limited to France, or at least to Europe, for his ballets never found favor in America. He was accused of collaboration with Nazi occupiers during World War II, or of consorting with Nazis, and he left his post as director of the Paris Opéra Ballet for a short period. He returned in the late 1940s and retained his association with the company for another decade.

Flamboyant and emotional, when he was a guest artist with the Ballet Russe de Monte Carlo in New York, he was suspected of dropping his partner, Alicia Markova, in a performance of *Giselle* because she received more applause than he did; he and Massine were supposed to fight a duel in Central Park; and in one of his many, many books he suggested that one could not expect to become an artist unless he were capable of pressing his mouth to the earth "in moments of madness."

Another boy marvel during Diaghilev's last years was Sydney Francis Patrick Chippendall Healey-Kay, English-born and trained, as were so many of the best English dancers, by Grace Cone and the Russian Seraphine Astafieva, headquartered in London. Patrick was a child-actor at first and made his first Diaghilev Ballets Russes appearance in the corps de ballet of *The Sleeping Beauty* under the name of Patrikéeff in 1921. But he returned later (1924–25, 1928–29) as a soloist. Roles in new ballets were created for him. Both he and Lifar were in Nijinska's *Le Train Bleu*; in

Dolin as a classical *danseur* early in his career.

Balanchine's *Le Bal*, he appeared with Lifar, Danilova, Doubrovska, and Balanchine; and in *The Prodigal Son*, he and the brilliant Woizikovsky danced the important roles of the Two Servants to Lifar's Prodigal. In these and other ballets he won instant recognition and, soon, fame abroad as well as at home, but neither as Healey-Kay nor as Patrikéeff. Instead, in 1923, a new name and a new star was born: Anton Dolin.

Dolin, from the start of his career and throughout his long dancing days (spanning more than

Markova and Dolin, the famous ballet team
of the 1930s, '40s, and '50s, in *Giselle*.

Dolin as Albrecht in *Giselle*, at the tomb of
Giselle at the end of the ballet.

forty years), never found any difficulty in shut-
tling between classical ballet and show business,
and although he was criticized, as was his most
frequent partner, Alicia Markova, for "debasing"
their art in revues in the early years, he brought
the elegance and discipline of ballet to the variety theater and, in turn, gave to ballet something
of the vitality and even flamboyance of the musical theater. In the 1920s and 1930s, he had little
choice but to go wherever there were jobs for
dancers. He was very adaptable. Especially admired were his acrobatic skills and choreographers were delighted to exploit these both in
ballet and in the commercial theater. Nijinska
made use of them in the role she created especially for him in *Le Train Bleu* and Markova,
reminiscing to an audience in the late 1970s, said,

Dolin today, coaching a student.

"Pat had remarkable feet. He could dance on his toes without toe shoes!"

Men in ballet do not, of course, dance *sur les pointes*—that is the province of the ladies of the ballet—but it could be suitable in character roles such as the devil in *Fair at Sorochinsk* (a 1943 ballet choreographed by David Lichine) or in virtuosic solos used both at all-ballet evenings and in music hall appearances. When, from a kneeling position, Dolin would roll upward onto full *pointe*, audiences applauded wildly in coliseums and opera houses. His popular *Bolero* (Ravel) might be performed with full orchestra, piano accompaniment, a recording, or with Larry Adler, the harmonica virtuoso, as his accompanist and because of its continuing popularity he saw no reason for not putting it in a repertory with *Giselle* or on a vaudeville bill, in rather the same way that the opera star, Grace Moore, might encore a concert featuring lieder with her popular rendition of *Ciribiribin* or the theme song from her movie, *One Night of Love*.

Hymn to the Sun (Rimsky-Korsakoff) was another popular Dolin solo and the dancer himself was as adept at partnering England's great musical comedy dancer Jessie Matthews as he was serving as the impeccable cavalier for the great ballerinas of four decades, most especially Markova. The acrobatics which Nijinska incorporated

into *Train Bleu* for him were suitable for a very contemporary ballet, yet Dolin could find perfectly valid reasons for incorporating such skills into the classics. In his first staging of *Giselle* for The Ballet Theatre (now the American Ballet Theatre), he had arranged a series of steps, a sort of stair, leading up to Giselle's tomb and at the very close of the ballet, when her ghost fades from view, Dolin, as Albrecht, raced up the stairs in a frenzy of passion, posed at the peak for a moment and then fell backward down the stairs and onto the floor. It was certainly not authentic— but how much of today's *Giselle* is, indeed, the Coralli-Perrot original?—but it was in keeping with the melodrama of the piece itself.

Dolin's itinerant status with the Ballets Russes in the 1920s was partly of his own choosing. He was ambitious and he had no intention of playing a secondary role in any ballet repertory, so when suitable parts were offered to him, he accepted. There were the inevitable rumors that he and Lifar were feuding, that each wanted to become the Diaghilev favorite. Dolin, speaking in the 1970s, refutes the rumors. "Serge and I got along very well," he says. "He was a brilliant dancer. He had his roles and I had mine and we danced successfully together. Truthfully, I was very relieved when Diaghilev selected Serge as his special protégé." Dolin, however, names Diaghilev (as does Markova) as a powerful and irreplaceable influence.

Diaghilev led Dolin, as he did so many others of his young artists, into a world of art far broader than the act of dancing itself. Dolin became a part of that surging Diaghilev enterprise that included the presences and the collaborations of great composers and painters, poets and librettists, avant-garde leaders in every aspect of theater. Dolin was not a pawn but a living part of those choreographic experiments that not only invigorated the dance of that era but also directed its participants toward new horizons. Dolin never became the celebrated choreographer that Fokine, Nijinsky (albeit aborted so young), Massine, and Lifar became, but from Diaghilev he learned more than the others, perhaps, about the art of building repertory, of assembling talent, of directing, and, most important, of guiding and molding his dancing successors.

Anton Dolin, while still very young, came to be recognized as the first English *premier danseur* of international stature in the history of ballet. "When Diaghilev died so unexpectedly," says Dolin, "we all felt that our world of ballet had died with him. It was a feeling worse than despair—it was just hopelessness, but then we knew that we had to gather up the pieces and start again. Serge went his way, other Diaghilev dancers made their moves on the continent, but we in England then began the business of building ballet in Britain." Dolin was instrumental in founding the Camargo Society, headed by Arnold Haskell and P. J. S. Richardson, in 1930, an organization that introduced a ballet subscription series. Young Markova and Dolin were among its junior stars. As far back as 1926, the Polish-born Marie Rambert had arranged ballet productions (one was commissioning Frederick Ashton to create his first choreography for a revue) for occasional presentation, but in 1930 the Rambert Dancers launched their first modest repertory season. The following year, Rambert and her associates founded the Ballet Club, which, like the Camargo Society, fostered young English choreographers, built repertories, presented promising dancers along with such established Russian stars as Karsavine or Lopokova. In 1931 a onetime

Diaghilev dancer, the Englishwoman Ninette de Valois (born Edris Stannus), who had established her own school and choreographic center in London, made a move through the Vic-Wells Opera to establish a British ballet company. It was the Vic-Wells Ballet that blossomed into the Sadler's Wells Ballet and ultimately into the Royal Ballet. Anton Dolin and Alicia Markova (Lillian Alicia Marks had joined the Diaghilev company at fourteen) were pioneers in all three of these key British ballet enterprises.

But in 1935 the Markova-Dolin Ballet was born, and although the two had danced together frequently in the past, this solidified a partnership which was to make them the most famous ballet "team" in the world, successors to Karsavina and Nijinsky and the brief but historic partnership of Anna Pavlova and Mikhail Mordkin, and predecessors of such dazzling partnerships as that of Margot Fonteyn and Rudolf Nureyev. The historic association was established through the Markova-Dolin Ballet of 1935–38 and again 1945–48 and Festival Ballet, established in London in 1950. The two in these associations were directors as well as partners but for the American dance scene they exerted their most potent dance influence as stars during the formative years of the American Ballet Theatre.

Each is possessed of a sturdy ego and each takes every possible opportunity to assert his own independent achievement in the world of dance. Yet as late as the fall of 1977, when they appeared together for the first time in twenty years, no longer dancers but performers still, a critic reviewing their mime excerpts from *Giselle* wrote, "the evening was a revelation . . . their unique power and chemistry returned intact . . ."

Dolin, his early acrobatic energies to one side, was a ballet virtuoso in his day. His elevation in *Le Spectre de la Rose* of the "Bluebird" *pas de deux* was commendable, he could do double air turns and three or four *pirouettes* (occasionally more) and audiences would gasp and cheer happily. But today's virtuosity is far more advanced (as it is for the ballerina) than that of the 1930s and '40s. A new kind of acrobatics, a balleticized gymnastic, came into Western ballet after Dolin had retired from his great classical roles. The

Bolshoi Ballet, emerging from the U.S.S.R. for its first tours, overwhelmed Western audiences with displays of physical prowess. What Dolin and his handful of male dance contemporaries had accomplished a decade earlier would have seemed tame by comparison. But in his era, Dolin was a first-rank *premier danseur*.

But if later *danseurs* have surpassed him in matters of physical prowess, no one has outclassed him as a partner. For all of his dancing decades, he was the dream partner, the hoped-for partner, for his gallant mien and deportment were impeccable and his actual physical support of the ballerina was strong, utterly dependable, seemingly effortless, and, most important of all, enhancing to the performance of his ballerina. Dolin knew that the function of the *danseur* was that of the cavalier, of the Prince Consort to the Queen of the Ballet. He "presented" his ballerina. He made her look good. "You may feel that your guts are about to spill out," he'll tell a young male dancer, "but you mustn't show it. Your partner may weigh a ton but you lift her as if she were lighter than air." Dolin lifted the world's greatest ballerinas, of all sizes and weights and shapes, and they were grateful to have him as their partner, but he was equally solicitous of unknown dancers making terrifying debuts. Before curtain time or during long last rehearsals, he would coach the novice in her role, help her and assure her, teach her useful tricks. Once on stage, he would transform the beginner into a "pro." More than one soloist became a star because Anton Dolin, unobtrusive and concerned, was literally behind her all the way.

With young male dancers, he was and remains equally solicitous and helpful. His coaching may often deal with the mechanics of partnering—of how to lift a girl (what happens to your knees? where should your hands grasp her body? how do you relate your timing to hers? how do you stop her at the end of a spin? etc.)—but his prodigious knowledge of period styles in ballet, of dramatic characterization through gesture and pacing, of filling a long musical phrase with meaningful or lyrical movement, has guided many a talented youth out of the gaucheries which held him back and into enactments distin-guished by polish and by stunning authority.

As a person, Anton Dolin—Pat to his close friends, Patrick (which he prefers) to most of his colleagues, Tony (the ladies especially love this familiar form of "Anton") to a few—has always been extrovert, outrageous if it amuses him to be so, endlessly restless, convivial in the extreme, possessed of a devastating wit that shoots like a rapier, loving and loyal despite his acid tongue, which he uses more for effect (as if delivering a line in a play) than for any desire to be cruel, and a joyous defier of convention, except in the presence of Britain's Royal Family, whose members he respects and adores.

But convention and protocol as such challenge his Irish belligerency. And even in communist countries, where he may travel to rehearse or coach one of his ballets (most often his brilliant restaging of the historic Victorian *Pas de Quatre*), he is perfectly capable of addressing a communist official as "baby," demanding services not programmed by the state, changing travel plans at the last minute, demanding champagne in flight on a socialist airline because it's his birthday (and he'll change the date to suit his desire for champagne) and acting as outrageously as possible, all with a bright twinkle in his eye.

Yet, he can be found backstage at a theater during a festival or ballet competition helping the young take that giant step that separates "execution" from "performing." In his mid-seventies, he'll show a seventeen-year-old who is learning the role of Albrecht how to fall or tell him that his hand is held behind him "not because some idiot told you to put it there" but because "the Wilis, invisible, are holding you back and you must show that mystical pull . . ." For nearly sixty years that "mystical pull" has served to draw a worldwide public, experienced dancers, newcomers, and students to Anton Dolin, a remarkable gentleman of the dance who has somehow managed to combine the elegance of a Louis XIV with the mischief of a leprechaun, the knowledge of a true pedagogue with the instincts of a circus acrobat, the vast ego of a great star with the selflessness of a parent, a dancing parent who cares more about the future of his dancing children than he does for himself.

7

FREDDIE
AND FRIENDS

THE INFLUX of great male dancers from Europe to the shores of America began in earnest with the coming of the Ballet Russe de Monte Carlo to America in the 1930s. There were brief preliminary impacts, however, when Nijinsky made an all-too-short tour in 1916 and when Mikhail Mordkin, Pavlova's virile and handsome partner, gave Americans a first startled and admiring look at male ballet dancers in 1910.

It was, however, the Ballet Russe de Monte Carlo under Massine (and with David Lichine as its first distinguished *premier danseur*) that became firmly rooted in America and it was here that one of the great men dancers of the era won his way to international stardom. This was Frederic Franklin, whose association with the Ballet Russe lasted, aside from a few brief interruptions, from 1938 to 1956. Franklin, born in Liverpool, began his career in cabaret. He could play the piano, sing and hoof; he partnered the darling of the French cabarets, Mistinguett, of the "million-dollar legs," in Paris, and he danced with Wendy Toye in English musicals, but England's Anton Dolin saw in the young man a potential dancer of ballet and gave him his first real chance as a classical dancer with the Markova-Dolin Ballet (he danced with that troupe from 1935 to 1937). When he came to the Ballet Russe de Monte Carlo in 1938, he was uniquely trained for what was then the most diversified and demanding repertory in all ballet. He was expected to dance the classics, romantic ballets, *demi-caractère*, character dances, modern ballets, jazz-oriented works, comedies, tragedies, abstract ballets, and even tap dancing. In all he excelled. He was, in-

deed, unique, and no male dancer in the history of ballet in America had ever before won a larger or more adoring public.

"From the time I was twelve up to seventeen with my second teacher, I had what was called musical comedy dancing. This included ballet, tap, elocution, and drama. It was an all-'round theater training. When I was ready to earn a living at seventeen there was no ballet company in England. There was nothing. But I was equipped to find a job in musical comedy . . . which I promptly did. The emphasis was certainly on ballet training and I did have to pass my examinations at the Royal Academy of Dancing, but for a job I needed the other techniques I had learned from my teacher. I was theater. I never had a Liverpool "Beatles" accent—that was stamped out of me as a child in my elocution and drama classes—because I was being totally trained for all kinds of theater.

"One of my first jobs was with the J. W. Jackson Troupe. And we did all kinds of routines. It called not only for tap dancing, which was the prime reason for the troupe itself, but also Spanish numbers, ballet, and I remember one bit where we did a routine on stilts as ducks! The group played the Casino de Paris and the star of the show was your own Josephine Baker! I was the dancer on the end of the line. My ballet technique was going to pot because I didn't know where to study in Paris. Later I found out that de

(Overleaf) Franklin today as Friar Laurence in a ballet version of *Romeo and Juliet*.
Michael Friedlander

Frederic Franklin in a pose from Sir Frederick Ashton's *The Devil's Holiday*, which was the first ballet Ashton did for the Ballet Russe de Monte Carlo, a company that toured the United States early in the 1930s, '40, and '50s.
Dwight Godwin

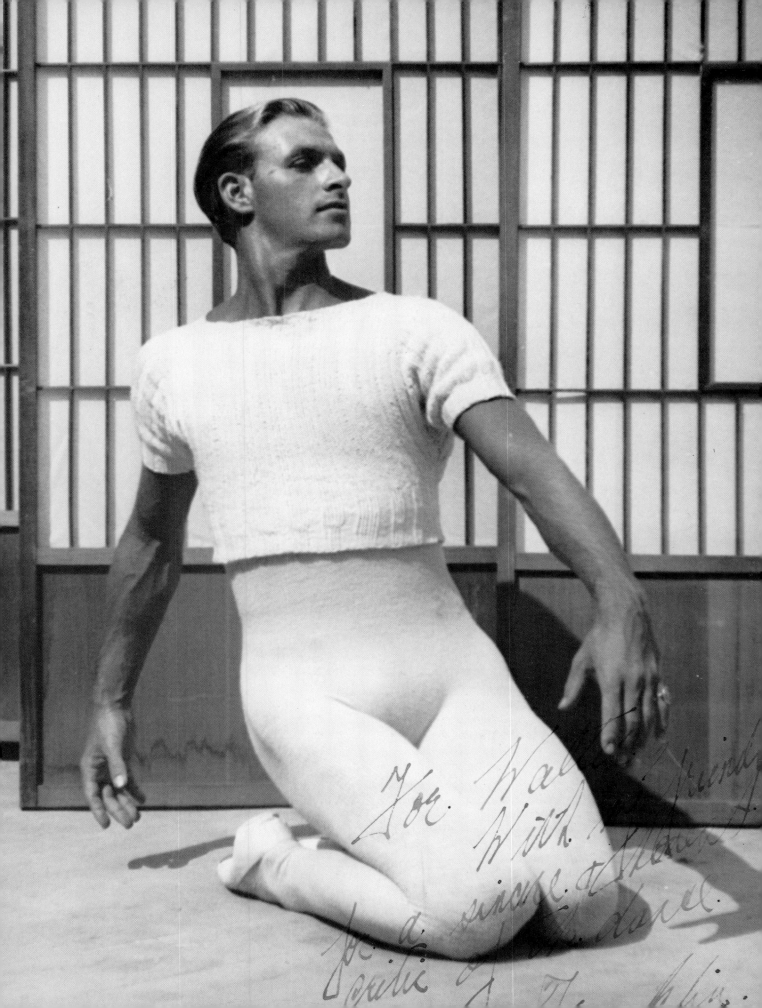

For Walt
With a sincere friend
Cecil [illegible]
[illegible]

The famous team of Franklin
and Danilova in *Gaité Parisienne*.

Basil was forming the Ballet Russe through auditions just up the street from Baker's studio and I'm sure if I'd known about it, I could have gotten a job, since men dancers were hard to find, but I was ignorant in 1931 at seventeen of the whole plan to found the Ballet Russe."

Instead, Freddie was playing the piano outside the boys' dressing room at the Casino. Mistinguett heard him, climbed the flight of stairs, and asked, in English, for the boy who played the piano. The singer on the show, Jean Sablon, was indisposed, so Mistinguett had teenage Freddie removed from the dance line, dressed in white tie and tails, sit down at the piano and play and sing "You're Driving Me Crazy" as the lovely star appeared, settled herself on top of the piano, and displayed those famous legs which had been insured—as the worldwide press had reported—for a million dollars.

Little Freddie looked back and thanked his stars that his teacher had stressed "the theatricality of dance." When he was still a boy in her school in the north of England, she had made routines for him and her other pupils and Freddie, sent off to North England competitions, won all sorts of medals. "What did we do in the competitions? Well, there were classical ballet sections, *demi-caractère*, character, and Greek interpretive dance, tap, musical comedy, and I was in all of them!"

In Liverpool and Blackpool competitions, he won top honors in two numbers: "I did a *demi-*

caractère number called—you'll die at the name!
—*The Satanic Serf* and I was dressed in a gray sort of wig which lit up! and in a musical comedy number I got the highest marks in the whole competition. I was bridging gaps all the way along. I was in the classical section and all else too. So I was ready for Mistinguett or Ballet Russe or anything theatrical!"

But in 1933, when dancing in cabaret with Wendy Toye, he saw the de Basil Ballet Russe and loved it. "But I had no intention at all of joining such a company, no intention of being a ballet dancer. I was a principal dancer in theater. Why would I want anything else? Of course, Wendy and I went to ballet class every day. Legat was our teacher. I studied with him the last three months of his life. I was eighteen and he said to Wendy's mother about me, 'This boy must work. He must train. He can be a ballet artist but it must happen now!' And then I went on to study with Kyasht and Sokolova. But I was performing in the theater all the time."

Franklin's childhood training and his teenage theatrical experiences were totally different from the hothouse atmosphere surrounding ballet dancers brought up in imperial, royal, and state ballet schools of other lands, Freddie learned to carry his show business aplomb over into ballet. In the mid-thirties, when he and Wendy were in support of Markova-Dolin and toured the English provinces, untutored audiences would "give us the bird," would boo and make wisecracks. "When I started cavorting about in tights—remember audiences in the provincial towns had never seen a man in tights—they'd scream. Or if Wendy would come on and look about as one does in ballet in search of the hero, someone would yell, 'There 'e is, dearie, over there!' and Wendy and I would come off stage in tears. But we kept at it. At eighteen, I learned to project."

In 1938, when Leonide Massine took over direction of the Ballet Russe de Monte Carlo and some of the dancers went over to de Basil and his newly organized Original Ballet Russe, Massine needed a new principal male dancer. He saw Franklin once in a supporting role with the Markova-Dolin Ballet, but with complete faith in the talent of the youngster, he engaged him as

premier danseur of the Ballet Russe de Monte Carlo. George Zoritch, a dancer so handsome that he was considered truly beautiful, had been engaged as principal, but an injury kept him off stage for some time and Franklin immediately inherited all principal roles, including parts especially created for Zoritch. Zoritch recovered and, attractive dancer though he was, never replaced Franklin as *premier*. For Frederic Franklin, on his American debut, was an instant hit, a star.

The "projection" Franklin acquired during his Casino de Paris and his English provincial tour appearances became a characteristic of his performances during his long career in America. His cabaret, vaudeville, radio (he was a child actor in a "Swiss Family Robinson" series), and musical comedy background did not place any stigma on him with his Russian colleagues in the Ballet Russe. For they too, with the death of Diaghilev, survived for a few seasons in revues and vaudeville until the Ballet Russe was re-formed.

So it was that when Frederic Franklin merely walked on stage as the handsome Baron in *Gaîté Parisienne*, every female heart in the audience beat a little faster, or when he played the mischievous, amorous Franz in *Coppélia*, his grin and his muscular exuberance seemed as lilting and lively as the effervescent Delibes music to which he danced. There were certain irresistible trademarks in movement. I remember the way he moved his head quickly, with the alertness of an animal, as if he wouldn't want to miss anything—the "anything," of course, was you in the audience. In *port de bras*, he had a way of reaching, as if a raised arm did not stop at the fingertips but extended itself invisibly far beyond the confines of the body to . . . of course, you in the audience. Characteristics such as these were projected through his innate rhythm and fine musicality—"my inner sense of rhythm and my musicality were gifts I was born with, but my theater training taught me how to use them."

From Dolin, the supreme partner for the ballerina, he learned not only the technique but also the gallantry inherent in partnering, and just as Markova and Dolin became one of the great ballet partnerships of the century, so did the team of Alexandra Danilova and Frederic Franklin work its magic through nearly twenty years of Ballet Russe de Monte Carlo and countless other associations, together with the short-lived Slavenska-Franklin Ballet, also a Danilova-centered troupe, and guest appearances around the world.

Franklin's versatility is awesomely apparent in a mere listing of ballets in which he appeared during his dancing career of more than fifty years. Over those years, for example, he has danced the rousing *demi-caractère Trepak*, the classical role of the Prince and the acting role of Drosselmeyer in *The Nutcracker*. He danced Albrecht in the greatest of romantic ballets, *Giselle*; the Prince in the greatest of classical ballets, *Swan Lake*; and the starring male role of the Champion Roper in the most celebrated of all Americana ballets, *Rodeo*. But add to these the Poet in *Les Sylphides*, the Hussar in *Le Beau Danube*, the sexy Favorite Slave in *Scheherazade*, the flashing Warrior in *Prince Igor*, both ebullient Franz and funny-wistful Dr. Coppelius in *Coppélia*, the waltz cavalier in George Balanchine's *Serenade*, and tough Stanley in *A Streetcar Named Desire*. Today, he is a first-class mime not only as Coppelius and Drosselmeyer, but also as Madge the witch in the old *La Sylphide*, Friar Laurence in *Romeo and Juliet*, the old Jewish father, Esdras, in Stuart Sebastian's ballet setting of Maxwell Anderson's *Winterset*. But no one will forget that he took on a truly "global" assignment as the Spirit of Creation in Massine's symphonic ballet, *Seventh Symphony* (Beethoven), and went about creating the world in only one movement of a four-movement symphony! And he made it wholly believable, but then Frederic Franklin has been both believable and magical throughout his dancing ("theatrical" dancing) days.

I asked Franklin if today's male dancers had greater virtuosity than those of his era. "Yes," he said, "but they have time to develop it and we did not." He went on to explain the "bone-breaking" tours of such companies as the Ballet Russe. "I hardly remember seeing my own company dance in those twenty years. I was always dancing myself! I'd often dance three ballets a night, and if there were a matinee, well . . . I'd do that too.

They were mostly one-night stands, hundreds of them, and our technique got chipped away. We all were impatient to get back to New York and go to class! And build back the technique as fast as we could, and then it was the tour again! Today's dancers don't know, thank God!, performing every day in a different city, riding trains or buses at night, hitting a strange theater, rehearsing, performing, traveling over and over again. We had technique, we had to, but today the dancers have time to build a better technique. And now I teach; it is my job to help this generation with all I've learned.

"When I was just beginning, my teacher got me into all the right ballet positions. Then she'd say, 'Now jump!' Next she'd say, 'While you're up there do you think you could turn around?' I'd try, and fall flat. I don't think she knew the term of *tour en l'air* but she was trying. Today, with all my own training and experience, I can help other boys to 'get up there and turn around' and each one, with a different body, has a different problem. So the teacher must analyze each body—even dissect it—to help the young dancer get there. The key to it all is *strength!*"

During his formative years, Frederic Franklin was guided by his first teacher, Mrs. Kelly; his second, Shelagh Elliot-Clarke, who entered him into all those competitions; Legat and other teachers of his early professional years and such stars as Massine, Dolin, Markova, and Danilova. From the stars he learned a great deal and he was strongly influenced by them, to the point of taking on certain of their performing mannerisms. One day, after a performance, Frederick Ashton came backstage and said to him, "All right, Fred, you've got it. Comb out all of that copying. You're not Dolin, you're not Markova. Comb them out of your dancing. You are you."

And Franklin, expressing his gratitude to all, did just that. But he need never have worried. When he was only seven years old, he had taken part in a recital in a theater in Liverpool. When the theater was being swept after the performance, a discarded program was found on the floor. By the number which Freddie had done was scrawled the prophetic words: "Freddie Franklin . . . a born dancer."

8

AMERICAN DANCE PIONEERS: NATIVE AND IMPORTED

Igor and André were born in Moscow—André the year of the Russian Revolution and Igor five years earlier—but both left home when only children. Neither expected to become a dancer. Igor Youskevitch, growing up in Yugoslavia, became an athlete, a gymnast, a member of Sokol, the famed Slavic calisthenics-gymnastics society founded in Prague in the mid-nineteenth century. Little André, rather frail, was given dancing lessons in Nice to build up his strength. By accident, or at least by a chain of fortuitous events, they became dancers; they became great dancers; they became the first Russian male dancers to become adopted sons of American ballet. For Igor Youskevitch and André Eglevsky not only became American citizens, they became *premiers danseurs* of American ballet companies.

The two were alike, since both excelled in the technique of classical ballet, yet unalike in build and in personal style. Igor was slender, almost slight, and a superb partner not just in the physical sense of supporting the ballerina but also in matters of gallantry, of an almost poetic concern for the ballerina. Technique was admirable; style superlative. Igor also had a way of instituting a movement phrase curiously like that of the modern dancer: he did not direct his feet to move

(Overleaf) Hugh Laing in Tudor's *Romeo and Juliet*.

sideways or forward and back; rather, he would lean into a movement with his body and his feet merely carried him to his goal. This gave his movement something of that quality described by Martha Graham as "the urgency to action."

André was noted for his brilliant footwork, his *batterie*, the multiplicity of his *pirouettes*. Of the two, he was the more spectacular virtuoso. A dozen *pirouettes* from a single preparation were not difficult for him and audiences waited breathlessly to see just how many he could pull off at a given performance. In lean periods, it was said that he'd lay bets on the number he could do, thus earning much-needed dollars. On at least one occasion, he was a happy (and rewarded!) winner with eighteen *pirouettes!* (Eglevsky's dancing ancestor, Auguste Vestris, you will recall, stunned his public with eight *pirouettes*.)

André also had elevation plus that quality that another of his dancing ancestors, Balon, gave to the vocabulary of ballet, *ballon*. For Eglevsky, who was built more or less like a football player in miniature, had the ability of suspending himself in air, or seemingly so. George Balanchine gave a choreographic frame to this *tour de force* on more than one occasion, but never better than in a solo for André in Minkus' *Pas de Trois* in which the *danseur* executed a *cabriole en avant* (with a soft clinging of the calves of the legs and no multiple beats) during which he actually seemed to be sitting in space with his legs stretched out comfortably in front of his body. He told me once that he actually "perfected the movement by sitting in a chair and lifting my legs off the floor. I practiced this over and over until it was easy. Then I simply did it without the chair." So famous was André for his virtuosity and, especially, his *pirouettes* that an audience of thousands at the old Metropolitan Opera House got an "in" joke when Jerome Robbins, for a gala, had André make an elaborate preparation for a multiple turn, and then do a single.

André, at fourteen, was dancing leading roles. Igor did not have a ballet lesson until he was twenty, yet in one year of intensive training, he was ready for his ballet debut. The body of a trained athlete, the flexibility and timing of a star gymnast, and participation in the 1932 Olympics

Alicia Alonso and Igor Youskevitch in George
Balanchine's *Theme and Variations* for the American
Ballet Theatre.
Fred Fehl

on the Yugoslav team had prepared him for a
new and unexpected career. Both André and Igor
received their principal ballet training in Paris.
André had come there after ballet studies in
Nice and Igor had come to partner the Yugoslav
dancer Xenia Grunt, who had urged a dancer's
career on him. Further encouragement came
from the celebrated Yugoslav ballerina Mia Slav-
enska, destined for a successful career in
America.

Unlike Dolin and Lifar, they were too young
to have danced with Diaghilev's Ballets Russes
but they did perform with the Monte Carlo
brand of Ballets Russes which emerged in the
early 1930s after Diaghilev's death. Their studies
found them seeking instruction in Paris, along
with most of their colleagues and contemporaries,
with three great ballerinas, now teachers, of Russian Imperial Ballet origins: Mathilde Kschessinska (the *prima ballerina assoluta* of the Impe-

rial Ballet), Olga Preobrajenska, and Lubov
Egorova. Igor was primarily a pupil of the much-
loved "Preo," and André, of the other two. There
were male teachers also, and André studied not
only with Nicholai Legat but also with Alexandre
Volinine, formerly *premier danseur* of the Bolshoi Ballet and, for more than a decade, Anna
Pavlova's partner.

Eglevsky came to America in 1937 and Youskevitch the following year. Both were principals
with the Ballet Russe de Monte Carlo and both
were cast in a variety of roles, but they were the
interpreters of the classics: *Giselle, Swan Lake*
(Act II was given as an entity in those days),
The Nutcracker (abbreviated), *Aurora's Wedding* (the last act of *The Sleeping Beauty*), and
such later classics in romantic style as *Les Sylphides* and *Le Spectre de la Rose*. Frederic Franklin, the third male principal, was principally
demi-caractère and an interpreter of new ballets; his essaying of traditional roles was stressed
at a later date.

Youskevitch and Eglevsky not only performed
the classics but they, too, in a decade of expanding, exploring repertory, introduced many new
roles, including the "symphonic ballets" of Mas-

sine. There may possibly have been feelings of rivalry among Franklin, Youskevitch, and Eglevsky and demands for premieres, new roles, billing, and the like, but whatever existed could not compare with the battles of the ballerinas in the 1930s. The gentlemen of the ballet were, at least on the surface, gentlemen. I remember once when, in a review, I found fault with the way Eglevsky was executing his *entrechats*. He telephoned me in an upset state and what he said, in remarkable candor and not quite fairly to himself, was: "Walter, Igor is the artist and I'm the virtuoso and if you take my virtuosity away what do I have left?" Later, when he had joined the New York City Ballet and came under the guidance of Balanchine, Eglevsky's inherent artistry came into balance with his immediately apparent physical prowess. But it was true in the Ballet Russe days that Igor was the better partner by far, the more tasteful and subtle performer.

While Franklin rose to his highest and broadest accomplishments with the Ballet Russe de Monte Carlo, Youskevitch and Eglevsky were to make their major impact in two American-born, American-oriented ballet companies. And with these later associations in their mature years and at the peak of their powers, they also made partnerships which, if not as long-lasting as that of Markova and Dolin nor quite as celebrated as the to-come partnership of Fonteyn and Nureyev, still made their marks in dance history. With the American Ballet Theatre (in those days simply The Ballet Theatre), Igor formed a historic partnership with Alicia Alonso; with the New York City Ballet, André and Maria Tallchief made magic together for a short but brilliant period.

Youskevitch was already a star with a devoted following when he succeeded Dolin in 1946 as *premier danseur* of ABT. Behind him was military service in World War II in the U. S. Navy and ahead were nine years with The Ballet Theatre, many of them with Alonso, whose seasons with the company were major but not continuous. It was during this decade that the team of Alonso and Youskevitch came to succeed that of Dolin and Markova as the matchless stars of *Giselle*, for although Markova continued to dance it with Dolin in other companies and

André Eglevsky in *Sylvia Pas de Deux.*

with many other partners (notably Erik Bruhn), Alonso-Youskevitch dominated the American scene in the classical sense, not only in *Giselle* but also in *Swan Lake* (Act II) and a variety of dazzling *pas de deux* (*Black Swan*, the *Bluebird*, *Don Quixote* among them) and in a major contemporary classic, *Theme and Variations*, which Balanchine created especially for them and ABT.

With the Ballet Russe, one would have seen Youskevitch as a god in the Elysian Fields scene (third movement) with Markova in *Seventh Symphony*—and here he moved with dignity, beauty, and a curious celestial lightness as if clouds were his pathways rather than earth—in *Rouge et Noir*, he wore a skin-tight costume that Matisse himself painted on the body, muscle-molding abstract designs on the otherwise unadorned body tights. With ABT, Youskevitch grew into one of the truly great *premiers danseurs nobles* of the century in the ballet masterpieces of the nineteenth century, but he also distinguished himself in contemporary ballets in the repertory of ABT. Almost startling was his success in Ballet Theatre's production of Bettis' *A Streetcar Named Desire*, for here his elegance and graciousness were replaced with the tough brutality necessary to the role of Stanley.

On one occasion, Igor's macho performance was not sufficient to match an impassioned performance by his co-star, Nora Kaye, dancing the part of Blanche. Just before the moment of ravishment, Igor stepped too close to Nora too soon, just as she launched herself into a turn with flailing arms. She caught him on the temple and knocked him out cold on stage. She improvised the rape scene over his inert body with commendable expertise and later, when she entered Sardi's for supper after the ballet, she asked for the reservation for "Butch Kaye."

After leaving ABT, Igor made guest artist appearances with several companies but with the 1960s he began to concentrate on teaching and on working with a semi-amateur group he founded called Ballet Romantique. Here, he launched another Youskevitch, his and Anna Scarpova's daughter, Maria, on her career in the world of ballet, partnering her with his familiar gallantry and a charming air of parental pride. With accuracy and aptness, the writer Selma Jeanne Cohen titled an article she wrote on Youskevitch, "Prince Igor."

Eglevsky, before becoming the *premier danseur* of the New York City Ballet in 1951, had made

Hugh Laing with Nora Kaye in Tudor's *Dim Lustre.*
Bob Golby

Jerome Robbins with Tanaquil LeClercq in *Bourrée Fantasque* by George Balanchine for the New York City Ballet.
Fred Fehl

his mark as a friendly rival to Youskevitch in classical parts with both the Ballet Russe de Monte Carlo and the American Ballet Theatre, as well as dancing principal roles in a variety of companies, the American Ballet (forerunner of the New York City Ballet), Blum's Ballets de Monte Carlo, de Basil's Original Ballet Russe, Massine's Ballet Russe Highlights, Ballet International, Grand Ballet du Marquis de Cuevas, and so on. He also danced in a Broadway musical and, in the movies, with Melissa Hayden in Charles Chaplin's *Limelight*. Ballets in which he created major parts were Massine's surrealist (with Salvador Dali) *Mad Tristan*, Fokine's *Helen of Troy*, the title role in ABT's revival of Balanchine's *Apollo*, the masterwork from the Diaghilev era.

With the New York City Ballet, Balanchine cast him in his new version of Act II of *Swan Lake*, interpolating a major male variation for

him; two dazzling *Pas de Trois*, the Minkus, with Tallchief and Kaye, and the Glinka with Hayden and Patricia Wilde; *Pas de Dix*, the most popular of all the excerpted *divertissements* from *Raymonda*, with Tallchief; *Scotch Symphony*, a plotless salute to the romantic *La Sylphide*, with Tallchief; the New York City Ballet's 1951 revival of *Apollo*, with Tallchief as Terpsichore; and that most brilliant of all Balanchine bravura duets (with the arguable exception of *Tchaikovsky Pas de Deux*), *Sylvia Pas de Deux*, with Tallchief.

The *Sylvia* became almost a trademark for the team of Tallchief-Eglevsky. They dressed in classical costumes, she with the short, powder-puff tutu and coronet, he as the cavalier, in powder blue. The steps? They demanded every bit of virtuosity these two virtuosi possessed, yet with all the physical demands, the moments of peril in swiftly timed spins and catches, aristocratic ease prevailed throughout. Here, in truth, was to be found the very essence of ballet prowess, distinguishing it from gymnastics: the difficult accomplished with ease; the near-impossible with aplomb; hazards with princely condescension.

André and Maria never failed to dance it with brightness, with an air of excitement, and with that perfection of technique which was frighteningly dependable. But I remember one performance at the old New York City Center that turned out to be incandescent. It was no special occasion—the company was simply midway in a repertory season—and *Sylvia Pas de Deux* was by this time a staple, a glorious staple of course but not a novelty. On this night something electrifying occurred. The dancers, as the saying goes, outdid themselves. But it was more than that. On stage there was perfection, not dull correctness, but perfection in step, musical phrase, spirit, an air of romance, even in the exhilaration of shining presences. The audience went wild and there was an incredible ovation. I fairly babbled in my review for the New York *Herald Tribune* and the always contained John Martin came as close to babbling with delight as was possible in his New York *Times* review. It was such a miraculous performance that I telephoned Tallchief the next day: "Maria, you know the *Sylvia* was a

Jerome Robbins in *Fancy Free* with Janet Reed.
Fred Fehl

triumph last night and I've got to know if you and André felt something special, something unusual or rare in your performance." The ballerina replied, "I know this is a chance for me to say something deep and quotable but I'll tell you exactly what happened. When the curtain closed on the *pas de deux* I said to André, 'It went very well, didn't it?' and he answered, 'Yes, it seemed to.' And that's all that happened as far as we were concerned." Three thousand people had felt differently, for seeing that performance of the *Sylvia Pas de Deux* they had had a rare glimpse of performing genius. The virtuosic eminence of Eglevsky has been described on more than one occasion, and in one word by his most celebrated partner, Tallchief: "Incredible!"

Hugh Laing, English-Irish and born in Barbados, was a very special kind of dancer in the world of ballet. He was not a classical dancer. Indeed, his classical technique was limited. He was not really a *demi-caractère* dancer nor a character dancer. But he was something special, something that had not existed before. He was a "dramatic" dancer, an actor-dancer, the brilliant exponent of male roles in ballets created by a very special kind of master choreographer, Antony Tudor. Not for him the Albrechts and the Siegfrieds of the old classics, nor the near-flawless technicians required by the abstract, non-narrative ballets.

When the blue portal curtains were violently wrenched apart in the Prologue to Tudor's *Romeo and Juliet*, Laing, in one tense step and an intense look, riveted the attention of the entire audience, his performing powers instantly at work. A Tudor dancer—and that is what Laing was—had to be concerned with the meanings of movement rather than either the virtuosic or purely pictorial values of step, stance, and gesture. In *Lilac Garden*, you would see Hugh take an *arabesque*. But it wasn't a pose. Rather like the runner on-the-mark, get-set, this was the choreographic preparation for an impassioned run. A turn in arabesque was not a pose given motion but a dramatic moment of indecision, of playing for time, of escape from the necessity of facing an issue, a person, a direction. This approach to the theater of dance within the framework of ballet was the particular genius of Tudor; the interpretation, the particular genius of Laing.

In the 1930s a dance dichotomy existed. The resurgent ballet and the newly emerged modern dance were not on good terms; indeed, they weren't on speaking terms. It was said that the two, because of totally different concepts, could never find a common meeting ground. Kurt Jooss, his company and his ballets, tried to find that ground. In England, Tudor, ballet-rooted, brought to his choreography the expressional powers of modern dance. Easily and to tremendous effect, he was able to fuse, say, movement of almost visceral depth with ballet's attitudes and arabesques. It was not as if he were creating a presumably utilitarian language like Esperanto but that he was extending an ancient vocabulary to include new words, new expressions essential to the choreographic voice of a new age. Hugh, from the very start, was the chief spokesman in this new language.

Hugh, at twenty-one, joined the Ballet Club in London in 1932. By 1934, as a member of Ballet Rambert, he was creating roles in such early Tudor works as *The Planets* and *The Descent of Hebe*. In 1936 came the role with which he would be most closely identified throughout his dancing career, the Lover in *Jardin aux Lilas* (*Lilac Garden*). The following year came *Dark Elegies*, closer to modern dance and ethnic-tinged ceremony than anything else in Tudor's repertory. Briefly, Tudor attempted to establish a London-based company with the American Agnes de Mille, but this was almost instantly replaced with the London Ballet, which he headed and with Laing as principal dancer. In 1939, Tudor and Laing joined the newly organized The Ballet Theatre (ABT) in New York and made their American debuts with the company's first performances in 1940.

The Tudor ballets, usually referred to as "dramatic" or "psychological" ballets to distinguish them from the "white" classical ballets, the fairytale ballets and the abstract ballets that were coming into view, provided Laing with matchless opportunities to display his quite unique talents as a dancing actor. He possessed comic skills, but the accent was on intense drama, sensual (even

sexual) force and, at times when required, a shivery quality of evil. His natural intensity was translated into ardor of the most passionate sort as Romeo or as the Lover in *Lilac Garden* and into almost dirty licentiousness in *Pillar of Fire*, the 1942 ballet that made Nora Kaye a star overnight and assured his own pre-eminence as the male interpreter of the new dramatic ballets. He could communicate an almost communal loneliness in Tudor's ritualistic *Dark Elegies* and an anguished personal loneliness, slashed with violence, as the Transgressor in *Undertow*.

Hugh was usually thought of and is remembered as "a Tudor dancer," and indeed he was for two decades, but he was also successful in roles in works by other choreographers, among these the

Rare photograph of Jerome Robbins rehearsing *The Prodigal Son* with Maria Tallchief. Looking on is George Balanchine, with Alexander Kopeikine at the piano.

Jerome Robbins, Alicia Markova, André Eglevsky, and Anton Dolin discuss Robbins' *Pas de Trois divertissement*, 1947.

scholarly Husband in Agnes de Mille's *Tally-Ho!*, the title role in Balanchine's *The Prodigal Son* (with NYCB), and the part of Harry Beaton in the Gene Kelly film version of *Brigadoon*. But among a kaleidoscope of dance images, one can never forget the figure in the dress uniform as he stands in eager anticipation of a clandestine touch, a swift and anguished embrace, a run of desperate urgency as he races toward his beloved knowing that union can be counted only in seconds, a stance of Victorian propriety beneath which one senses the presence of passionate TNT that a spark, a touch, a glance could ignite.

Jerome Robbins is a choreographer. The dance world thinks of him as a choreographer, one of the greatest America has ever produced. But Jerry was also a dancer. Whether he belongs among the great male dancers of ballet is highly debatable, but what is inarguable is that he has given some great performances in very special roles in which he excelled.

I remember Jerry in his very first corps de ballet performances with The Ballet Theatre.

69

Jerome Robbins in *Tyl Ulenspiegel*, a ballet created for him by George Balanchine.

Jerry did. He also created the role of the apple-chewing, yarn-knitting Hermes in the comedy-ballet *Helen of Troy*, conceived and partially choreographed by Fokine and completed by David Lichine following Fokine's death. Later Kriza and still later Eliot Feld played Hermes with great success, but Jerry was the first . . . and the best.

His remarkable comic gifts—the faultless timing of gesture, of a knowing glance, a take and a double-take—were also present in his dancing of the amorous Youth in de Mille's *Three Virgins and a Devil* and in the first movement of Balanchine's *Bourrée Fantasque*, during the course of which long-legged Tanaquil LeClercq, standing in *front* of him surreptitiously kicked him in the *back* of the head. It was a funny movement but Jerry's response to it was essential to its wit. Again, no one else ever danced this role so deliciously.

Dramatic roles were also well within the range of Jerry's performing artistry. He brought not only the surface restlessness but also the deep emotional urgency to the part of the Son in the New York City Ballet's 1950 revival of Balanchine's *The Prodigal Son,* and Balanchine created especially for Robbins' actor-dancer skills a remarkable ballet, never a popular favorite but a brilliant choreographic exposition of myth, history, and sociopolitical commentary, *Tyl Ulenspiegel* (inspired by Richard Strauss's music, "Till Eulenspiegel's Merry Pranks"). The character of Tyl (or Til or Till) had, of course, inspired Nijinsky to create his last ballet and, after Balanchine-Robbins, the French virtuoso Jean Babilée to choreograph such a ballet for himself. But the Robbins Tyl must go on the record as a lost but not forgotten masterpiece of dance acting.

Technically, he was not nearly as polished as some of the other boys, but I found myself drawn to the way he moved even when he fell off a *pirouette*—Jerry *danced* his errors while others simply *executed* steps, no matter how correctly. In his own first major choreography, *Fancy Free*, he created the role of the sailor whose variation is a rumba and who dances the wistful, fresh, tender jazz *pas de deux*. In both he was superb and if John Kriza (another sailor of the original cast), who inherited the *pas de deux*, was as charming in it as was Jerry, no one ever gave the rumba the same irreverent undulation and gluteal fillips that

John Kriza is special. He is also historic. For Johnny, in his modest yet incredibly versatile way, made dance history by becoming the first American male dancer in classical ballet to win international recognition. America's John Durang and George Washington Smith of the eighteenth and nineteenth centuries, respectively, were not known beyond the United States. Juba (William Henry Lane), though triumphant abroad, was a tap dancer, albeit "the king" of dancers in this realm, and Ted Shawn was the first American male dancer to become world famous, but he was an innovator, a pioneer of new movement discoveries. Johnny Kriza, though excelling in an awesome repertory of dramatic roles in ballet, was classically trained, a Siegfried in *Swan Lake*, a Poet in *Les Sylphides*, a dashing cavalier in the *Grand Pas de Deux* from *Don Quixote*, the hero Colin (or Colas) in the world's oldest international ballet, *La Fille Mal Gardée*.

Johnny, born of Czech parents in Berwyn, Illinois, right outside of Chicago, studied first in Berwyn and then in Chicago with Bentley Stone and Walter Camryn, two of the most influential dancers, choreographers, and teachers in the Middle West. His dancing debut on a professional level took place when he was nineteen with the Chicago Opera Ballet, then directed by Ruth Page, a major figure on the American, and international, ballet scene. Johnny, who had begun his lessons in dancing at five with Mildred Perchal in Berwyn, was later described by the powerful Chicago critic Claudia Cassidy as "Mr. Ballet Theatre." He came to symbolize the dancing virility of ABT's celebrated male contingent during his twenty-six years with the company, was praised by heads of state as well as by international critics, for Johnny's lusty yet sensitive dancing did not go unnoticed (nor uncommented upon) by such as John F. Kennedy; Nikita Khrushchev of (the U.S.S.R.) the country that has long considered itself the capital of the ballet world, and by Her Majesty Queen Elizabeth II. Party Chairman Khrushchev praised Kriza for his dancing of the title role in Fokine's last ballet, *Bluebeard*; President Kennedy went for *Billy the Kid*; the Queen responded warmly to Johnny in *Fancy Free*.

John was very much the star exponent of the new age of ballet, the age of dramatic dance, of Americana, of jazz rhythms in ballet. Roles were created for him in these genres, or he would take over roles, such as Billy in *Billy the Kid*, and make them his own for his generation. But unlike Hugh Laing, who was essentially a Tudor dancer, or Robbins, who was both a dramatic dancer and *demi-caractère*, Johnny also excelled in the clas-

sics, especially as a partner. In the classical wing, his teacher and coach when he joined The Ballet Theatre in 1939 as a charter member for the troupe's debut in 1940, was Anton Dolin. It could be said that Dolin groomed Johnny in the classics from *corps de ballet* status to principal.

Johnny and Alicia Alonso were the harbingers, in a new version of the *Don Quixote Pas de Deux*, of the spectacular lifts that the Bolshoi Ballet would subsequently export. There was an overhead lift and a drop of the ballerina almost to the floor. Audiences gasped. I asked Johnny where he and Alicia had learned it. He laughed and said, "It's just got to be Lithuanian, hasn't it?" They had indeed learned it from a Riga-born Russian-trained teacher. Alonso, Cuban, was perfect for *Don Q*, of course, and Kriza, slender, dark-haired, and exuberant, was her match in communicative Spanish bravado, ballet style.

To the Prince in *Swan Lake* (the Act II production), he brought that elegance of mien, that gallantry for the ballerina that Dolin had taught him combined with his own directness of manner, his cleanness of gesture, sans flourishes, which seemed distinctly American. Fokine, of course, was with the company in its first seasons, so Kriza learned the Fokine style too and this, when he graduated from corps roles to soloist and principal, gave him ease in lyrical, romantic assignments. Tudor was there also to influence him, if not to guide him, along with Agnes de Mille, who taught him much about comedy timing and gesture, and Eugene Loring, who directed him in *Billy the Kid*. His dancing colleague and contemporary Jerome Robbins was the first to create especially for him: for his body, his way of moving, his own personality, his gentleness, his humor—this resulted in the role of the easygoing, good-natured Sailor No. 2 in *Fancy Free*.

All of these schoolings, trainings, influences, directings, and choreographings provided the young dancer with an enviable array of dance tools with which to make an image for himself and of himself. The talent was there—that uniqueness with which everyone is born but which is rarely developed—and Johnny used those tools given him to sculpt the new and unique American dance artist. His remarkable versatility was a mirror of the character of the repertory in which he performed, for The Ballet Theatre then and now was and is dedicated to rich diversity.

It would be inaccurate, however, to say that John Kriza was primarily a classical dancer or that he was a true *danseur noble*, for although he was accomplished in all ballet assignments, he was matchless in roles that challenged and probed his dramatic skills, his emotional depths, his genuine gaiety of spirit. Loring, of course, long danced the title part in his *Billy the Kid* and he was superb in it. Michael Kidd was top-rate too, as much later Eliot Feld would be. But no one ever revealed the vulnerability, as well as the overt bravado, of Billy as well as Kriza did. It was a dashing characterization but it was also a profound one.

In *Fancy Free*, as the nicest guy among the three sailors, as the gob who could be a poet while being a toughie, he was irresistible. All artists are replaceable and, in due course, John had to be replaced, and by excellent dancers, but he was never equaled. As the Pastor in de Mille's *Fall River Legend*, the melodrama of Lizzie Borden, he was required to do very little formal dancing but his was the role of compassion in a dance-drama about violence and murder. The Pastor was stalwart in body and in spirit. In de Mille's *Tally-Ho!*, there was nothing stalwart about John's playing of the satiated Prince. You could knock him over with a feather. In Herbert Ross's *Caprichos*, based upon Goya's own biting commentaries to his etchings of the same name, Kriza captured the inner terror, the emptiness, the awful decadence, the doomful nature of the Goya concept in his dancing (with his frequent partner, Ruth Ann Koesun) in a macabre, terrifying duet . . . he danced with, manipulated, was weighed down by, trapped, tentacled by an inert female body, with dead, flailing arms, legs, head, and a cascade of long, loose hair. He was partner here to a living death, to mortification that would not go away.

In William Dollar's *The Combat* (or *Le Combat* or *The Duel*), he pranced, fought, dueled, and loved on imaginary horseback as the Crusader warrior Tancred, and in de Mille's *Rodeo* he galloped, roughhoused, roped, and wooed as the tap-dancing Champion Roper. To paraphrase, and reverse, an old saying, he was a jack of all roles and master of all. In 1966, after more than a quarter of a century with ABT, the still boyish Johnny felt the time had come to retire. There was no Gala Farewell. One night, at the New York State Theater, he danced the Pastor in *Fall River Legend* and at intermission came to the promenade-bar level for a drink. He looked around for me, found me, and said, "I just wanted you to know that I just made my farewell. I haven't even told Lucia [Lucia Chase, head of ABT] yet. You've always been good to me. You've always liked my dancing. You were always encouraging. I wanted to tell you first. I'm not going to say anything to any of the other critics . . . if you thinks it's news, it's all yours . . . but whatever . . . thanks again."

Nine years later, in 1975, he died in a drowning accident. He had his gala tribute then, for the dance world congregated for his funeral in Chicago. In Los Angeles, West Coast dancers held a service for him. In New York, Lucia Chase arranged for a church service that did not mourn his passing so much as it celebrated his dancing life. And with unheard-of speed for an institution, the Dance Collection of the New York Public Library assembled a John Kriza Exhibition of photographs spanning his entire life (including rare snapshots taken by Jerry Robbins), his first contract with Ballet Theatre, and, from *Fancy Free*, his sailor hat all by itself . . . Johnny was gone . . . we all wept.

"I'm a very brutal person," said soft-spoken, effervescent Leon Danielian. "If I don't like what you're wearing, I'll tell you. I cannot help it. But I'm just as brutal about myself. Years ago, I looked at my nose. I didn't like it. I had a hunk of it cut off. In *Giselle* when I walked onto the stage, I didn't feel I looked like Albrecht. I love myself but my image of myself wasn't that. I danced Albrecht but it offended me . . . I'm an esthetic person . . . I was a *demi-caractère* dancer with a classical technique. I felt that I had been tapped for an important place in ballet. I was

presented with a fascinating variety of roles but I had to find me. I did."

The gentle "brutality" went on. "I'm nearly fifty-eight. How much more time do I have? Why not tell the truth. I started my professional ballet career in 1937 with Mordkin. He was a dreadful teacher, simply dreadful! That's the truth so why not set the record straight. But to be honest, he did bring great love of ballet to his students and a love of theater too. But he couldn't teach. I didn't find that even Fokine taught me much in technique. Dolin did. He asked me if I could do *entrechat-huit*. I said I guessed so and did it. But he taught. He helped with body placements. He knew how to teach. I learned a lot. I owe him a great deal. All of us boys in the first years of Ballet Theatre learned a helluva lot about classical dancing from Dolin."

Leon's dancing career began in Red Bank, New Jersey, where he and his sister performed on vaudeville stages before the showing of silent films. The children were supposed to do dances somehow connected, no matter how tenuously, with the film to follow. Leon remembers that one movie had a Russian theme so that he was expected to do a Russian dance with *prisiadkas*, those deep-knee-bend bounces and kicks, and that a delay in the showing of the movie had him

breaking all *prisiadka* records! There was no early "call" to be a dancer, no vision. "I came from an Armenian family where the children did what they were told to do by their parents. My mother had an Armenian-Russian friend who taught ballet so she told my sister and me that we'd take ballet lessons. So we did. That's how I became a dancer."

The family was poor. Father was an Armenian born in Turkish-controlled territory. Mother was Armenian born in Tiflis, the Georgian city that produced George Balanchine, choreographer; Vakhtang Chaboukiani, *premier danseur*; Rouben Ter-Arutunian, theater designer. Leon was born in New York but lived for a few years in Atlantic Highlands, New Jersey. Mme. Seda (Suny), Tiflis-born, journeyed to Jersey once a week to give ballet lessons to Leon, his sister, and others. "I don't know what all the neighbors thought of *battements tendus* on the front porch. Mme. Seda was a wonderful teacher. Viola Essen was her pupil and, later, Jacques d'Amboise. She helped my sister and me with our vaudeville act and we premiered it in Red Bank."

Later, Leon and his sister, when the family moved back to New York, were available for bar mitzvahs, Greek weddings, Spanish fiestas. "I remember we'd go to upper Broadway with our

'Jewish' numbers as we called them. My father would take me to the men's room of a meeting hall and I'd put on the little cap, the shawl, and do a number. Next day, we'd get decked out in Mexican costumes and do 'La Camparasita,' and of course we did Armenian numbers. We did anything we were asked to do. We'd take on anything."

From 1933 to 1937 the little Danielians "were ready for all ocasions." Then came the Mordkin Ballet, where Leon first met Lucia Chase, then a principal dancer with the troupe, a Broadway show (*I Married an Angel*, choreographed by Balanchine and starring the then Mrs. Balanchine, Vera Zorina), and The Ballet Theatre from its moment of organization in 1939 through 1941. The year 1942 was spent with de Basil's Original Ballet Russe, and from 1943 to 1961 he was associated as either permanent or guest artist star with the Ballet Russe de Monte Carlo.

Danielian (for a year he was billed as Danieloff and hated it), a year younger than Kriza, made a name for himself in classical parts before Johnny, thus becoming the first American classical dancer of nationwide renown in this century. "I'm too modest to have said this myself," he remarked, "but I'd be grateful if you would say I was the first American *premier danseur* of this era, the first to come along, because it's fact. Later, it was Johnny and me. There were other American male classical dancers but we two were known internationally."

Leon said he thought one should say that there was a triumvirate of young American male stars of the early forties but that the third was "unfulfilled." This, of course, was the spectacular Canadian-born Ian Gibson of the short and dazzling career that came to an abrupt end because Ian's military service had interrupted his dance training at a crucial time. Although he tried to retrain after World War II, his body said "too late." But Leon, the most celebrated American "Bluebird" of that period, went to see Ian's first *Bluebird*. Leon's reaction was instant: "I knew then I was a ballet fan. He was terrific. I never thought about my *Bluebird* at all. I just clapped and shouted for his." Ian, with incredible elevation and *ballon*, was a soaring "Bluebird" in the

famous *pas de deux* from *The Sleeping Beauty*. Dancing Alain, the semi-idiot bumpkin in *La Fille Mal Gardée*, he had audiences gasping as he chased butterflies while suspended in air. His *Le Spectre de la Rose* invited comments by those who had seen Nijinsky, and Ian fared well in comparison. Ian felt he had to stop. Leon and Johnny went on.

Leon's first success came in 1940 when Dolin, staging Act II of *Swan Lake* for Ballet Theatre, interpolated the *Pas de Trois* from Act I, thus giving Leon the role of Benno, the Prince's friend, and also an opportunity to display his remarkably bright and glittering *batterie*, his marvelous lightness, the exuberant allegro style for which he became famous. His Spanish routines from vaudeville days stood him in good stead for *Goyescas* and Andrée Howard's dramatically effective but unappreciated ballet *Lady into Fox* gave Leon a stunning role as the Huntsman. The Nijinsky roles in both *Les Sylphides* and *Carnaval* (Harlequin) came his way.

But it was with the Ballet Russe de Monte Carlo that Danielian was given endless opportunities to display his versatility. He succeeded Massine as the Peruvian in *Gaité Parisienne* and made the part his own. You could have seen him as either the King of the Dandies or the Hussar in *Le Beau Danube*. *Carnaval, Sylphides, Bluebird* were again his, along with the *Black Swan* and *Don Quixote Grand Pas de Deux* and *The Nutcracker pas de deux* (in which he hated himself). With his "brutality" of criticism, he also added *Spectre* to parts he danced but which he felt were wrong for him, and as for Nijinsky's *The Afternoon of a Faun*, Danielian described himself as "dreadful, just dreadful!" And then goes on to say, "In *Madroños* I had a one-minute solo that brought down the house . . . and deservedly!" With Danilova he danced the premiere of the Ballet Russe's production of Balanchine's *Danses Concertantes*, and when he worked briefly as guest star with the San Francisco Ballet for that company's State Department-sponsored tour of the Orient, he added that special repertory to his own extensive roster of roles.

Since Danielian, for his era, was a virtuoso, it is interesting to hear his opinions of today's vir-

John Kriza with Ruth Ann Koesun in the ballet *Caprichos* by Herbert Ross.

great roles, so my repertory was really enormous. I was lucky because here I was in all kinds of ballet companies, in musicals, in vaudeville, in night club acts, dancing with Yvette Chauviré in France and someone else in Japan, doing my so-called 'Jewish' dances and my Spanish dances and my Armenian dances. So from the time I was four years old, I was doing the only thing I knew how to do, to dance."

Since 1968, Leon Danielian has been director of the American Ballet Theatre School. He has made the school a success—"I never thought I'd be interested in electric light bills but I am!"—both administratively and educationally. He continues as a major teacher at that school and, especially for his classes for boys, endeavors to give his charges the knowledge he has stored up from a repertory ranging from "garbage to masterpieces" and from a long stage career that never lost sight of the fact that "ballet is theater, or should be."

Painful arthritis never downed him for long, despite major operations, and naturally he has been unable to dance since the mid-1960s. But the nineteen-year-old who obliged Dolin with an *entrechat-huit* these many years ago, says, "I think with a good *plié* and my two plastic hips I could still do *entrechat-huit*, maybe even *entrechat-dix!*" For Leon Danielian, American ballet "pioneer" (as he thinks of himself), could always do anything asked of him.

These gentlemen of the dance were indeed pioneers on the American ballet scene. They were not entirely alone. The handsome, dashing, sexy Yurek Shabelevsky of Polish extraction was a bright comet soon gone. Roland Guerard provided a touch of American classicism to the Ballet Russe. And the three Christensen brothers—Lew, Willam, Harold—gave the public glimpses of ballet when there were no American ballet companies to provide the glimpses; out of vaudeville they came to serve ballet in America, with Lew the pioneering leader as the major male principal in the early efforts of Balanchine in America.

Along with Leon Danielian, they "did everything," and that included bringing honor and distinction to the male dance in America.

tuosi: "We didn't dance in 1940 like the boys do now, doing your special tricks. We danced like the men did before us in the roles we inherited and presumably they did them as the choreographers intended for them to be danced. You didn't insert your own special trick just to bring the house down. It really is not kosher; it's very exciting but it isn't right. In those days, if you changed things you were criticized. But the tricks of technique weren't necessary if you knew theatrical tricks. I learned from watching Markova, for example. She knew her theater. She knew when to do what, what lights she was moving in—Loie Fuller and Ruth St. Denis knew that too—and I liked that because I believed then and now that it's all theater.

"I had a few dances created for me, but that was rare. I danced all the garbage as well as the

9

THEIR MAJESTIES' DANCERS: THE UNITED KINGDOM; THE KINGDOM OF DENMARK

Cᴇʀᴛᴀɪɴ of His Britannic Majesty's *danseurs*, in the 1930s and '40s, elected to seek their dance fortunes in the New World, as their forebears, the colonists and settlers, had done three centuries before. Thus it was that Anton Dolin (for a period of time) and Frederic Franklin, Antony Tudor, and Hugh Laing (permanently) became key figures in the renascence of ballet in America and, indeed, in the development of ballet destined to take on a distinctly American cast.

But what of the homeland? What about a renascent English ballet? A trio of strong women, Lillian Baylis (a supporter of ballet through her Old Vic and Sadler's Wells theaters) and Ninette de Valois and Marie Rambert (organizers-directors as well as choreographers and onetime dancers) made possible the firm establishment of British ballet. And such creative talents as Tudor, soon to leave for America, and Frederick Ashton, who would bring choreographic glory to ballet in England, were nurtured by these splendid ladies. But what of performers? There were ballerinas, either in fact or in healthy incipiencies, but what about great male dancers? Except for Dolin there were none of international renown. Yet if there were to be great British ballets there had to be first-rank male dancers. World War II played havoc with male dance potential. Incipiencies, killed, maimed, thwarted, or too-long postponed, could not become fulfillments. The precious few survivors made possible the evolution of the first truly British ballet and the birth of the first "Royal" ballet in the history of the British Isles. (The first "Royal" ballet in the British Commonwealth and Empire was Canada's Royal Winnipeg Ballet.)

The two major male dancers of international stature in the developing days of the Royal Ballet (then the Sadler's Wells) and on its first trip to America in 1949 were Robert Helpmann and Michael Somes. The Australian-born Helpmann began his ballet training in his homeland, where he studied with Laurent Novikoff, Pavolva's partner during the ballerina's tours there in the early 1920s. For several years he danced in Australia but traveled to England in 1933, where he joined the Sadler's Wells Ballet, then the Vic-Wells. He was twenty-four at the time, but served only in the *corps de ballet* and continued his studies at the company school. That year, he was given his first solo in de Valois' *Job*, which starred Dolin as Satan. But when Markova and Dolin left the Wells in 1935 to form their own company, the time was auspicious for the birth of two new stars and the founding of a new ballet team. The preceding year, fifteen-year-old Peggy Hookham had become a member of the *corps de ballet*. Her first appearance was in *The Nutcracker*; her first role, the young Tregennis in *The Haunted Ballroom*. The next year, 1935, this teenager, who had taken the name of Margot Fonteyn, replaced Markova in most of her roles. Helpmann became the replacement for Dolin.

Helpmann remained with the company as *premier danseur* until 1950, when he left to concentrate on a career in acting, one which he pursued

(Overleaf) Robert Helpmann with Margot Fonteyn, very early in the days of the Vic-Wells Ballet.

Michael Somes with Margot Fonteyn in *Firebird*.

John Gilpin, outdoors in a classical pose.

with tremendous success. But for his fifteen years with the Wells, he and Fonteyn led the company to fame at home and triumphs abroad. As the company's *premier*, he did, of course, dance the great classical roles—Albrecht in *Giselle*, the Princes in *Swan Lake* and in *The Sleeping Beauty*, *Les Sylphides*, Franz in *Coppélia*—but his forte was dramatic dance. His first major role, a part he created, was the Master of Tregennis in *The Haunted Ballroom* and he went on to star in other ballets choreographed by de Valois: *Checkmate*, *The Prospect Before Us*, *Orpheus and Eurydice*; and Ashton ballets, among them, *Apparitions*, *Les Patineurs*, *A Wedding Bouquet*.

Helpmann's strength lay in his skills as an actor-dancer. In this category, he danced (or played) the title role in his fantasia on *Hamlet*, in *Miracle in the Gorbals*, *Comus*, and *Adam Zero*. It was a foregone conclusion, therefore, that he would eventually phase out his dancing and turn to acting. His Oberon in *A Midsummer Night's Dream*, with Vivien Leigh as Titania, played the Old Vic in London, and with Moira Shearer as Titania, he performed in New York and on tour. With Shearer, he starred in two major ballet-oriented films, the spectacularly successful *The Red Shoes* and *Tales of Hoffmann*.

The 1960s and '70s have seen Sir Robert (knighted by Queen Elizabeth) as actor, director, choreographer, and mime. He has directed the Australian Ballet and he is never too far from the world of ballet to return for the mime role of Carabosse in *The Sleeping Beauty*, to dance the Tango in Frederick Ashton's *Façade*, or even to join Sir Frederick in *Cinderella*, where the two "Sirs" have a ball playing the roles of the two Ugly Sisters.

Helpmann was never the virtuoso in technique —although he was a true virtuoso as mime and actor—that today's male ballet stars have become. But during the early days of the company that was to become the Royal Ballet, he carried the principal roles in the male wing almost single-handedly and because of him, together with Fonteyn, British ballet gained an eminence it has never lost.

Michael Somes, the first boy to win a scholarship at the Sadler's Wells Ballet School (in 1934, when he was sixteen), served in World War II, as did most of his seniors (Harold Turner and William Chappell among them) and his contemporaries. Although he was seriously injured, his dancing body recovered from the debilitation of military service more readily than did those of his elders, and this, coupled with his superior natural gifts, made him Britain's finest male dancer of the immediate postwar period. He created his first leading role in Ashton's *Horoscope* in 1938. After the war, Somes began dancing with Margot Fonteyn and, with the retirement of Helpmann,

Maria Tallchief and Erik Bruhn in
Miss Julie, the Birgit Cullberg ballet.
Jack Mitchell

Erik Bruhn as James, the hero, in *La Sylphide*.
Martha Swope

Erik Bruhn as Madge, the witch,
in La Sylphide.
Martha Swope

Erik Bruhn as Madge in
La Sylphide, with
Rudolf Nureyev as the hero.
Linda Vartoogian

became not only the *premier danseur* of the company but also Fonteyn's most frequent partner, a "team" that dominated British ballet until the great ballerina formed a partnership in 1962 with Rudolf Nureyev, which for a decade was the most publicized that the world of dance had ever known.

Somes, handsome, elegant of mien, and technically polished, danced the great classics—*Swan Lake, Giselle, The Sleeping Beauty*—with Fonteyn. But it was his good fortune to create new roles in new ballets, usually with Fonteyn, and here he excelled. In Ashton's *Daphnis and Chloe*, the best of the current versions of the Ravel masterpiece, he was dashing, ardent, and incredibly handsome, in face and in figure, as Daphnis. He was the romantic, impetuous, anguished lover Palemon in Ashton's full-length *Ondine*, a stunning ballet created especially for Fonteyn; Amyntas, the shepherd-hero of Ashton's three-act *Sylvia* (for Fonteyn); Prince Ivan in a revival of *Firebird*; co-star with Fonteyn in the abstract *Symphonic Variations* of Ashton; and the Elder Germont, an acting role, in Ashton's *Marguerite and Armand*, Ashton's poetic fantasia of the Camille story for Fonteyn and Nureyev. Aside from occasional mime roles, he has served as an assistant director of the Royal Ballet (1963–70) and as a principal teacher of the Royal Ballet School and a valuable *répétiteur*.

Somes had just retired when Nureyev blazed onto the British dance scene, but David Blair had not. Blair was the logical successor to Somes as Fonteyn's partner and, indeed, he served in that capacity on Somes's retirement in 1961. But barely had a year passed when the prestigious Dame Margot (made a Dame of the British Empire in 1956) introduced the defecting Russian to the British public and shortly thereafter made him her almost inseparable partner.

Blair, like Somes before him, had won a scholarship to the Royal Academy of Dancing and his teachers soon recognized his great promise. That promise was fulfilled when he joined the Sadler's Wells Theatre Ballet (the second company of the Sadler's Wells) in 1947 at fifteen. His rise was swift. He danced soloist roles from the start,

Bruhn as the Saracen in the American Ballet Theatre's *Raymonda*.
Linda Vartoogian

created the role of Captain Belaye in Cranko's *Pineapple Poll* when he was only eighteen; moved up to the Sadler's Wells Ballet itself in 1953 as soloist and in 1955 became a principal. The next giant step was as Dame Margot's partner in 1961; a year later it was all over. No, David Blair did not retire, but he had been replaced. He was still *premier danseur* of the Royal Ballet but the dazzling guest artist, a permanent guest it turned out, made him so secondary that, splendid dancer though he was, he seemed only a routine principal. Nureyev had come not only to outshine Blair but also every other male dancer, with the exception of Erik Bruhn, in the Western ballet world.

Blair, understandably, was bitter. He said to me: "I just don't understand it. You and the

other critics were praising me, encouraging me, seeing in me the most accomplished male dancer with the best technique that England had produced. Now suddenly I'm completely overlooked and by . . . Nureyev!" How could you tell him that although he had become a principal, he had never quite become a star and that he had been eclipsed not simply by one who was a star but a superstar at that. True, he could do almost anything in matters of technique that Nureyev could do, but he could not do it the way that Nureyev did. How could one tell a fine *danseur* that to see Nureyev walk on stage, stand still, or take a curtain call was more exciting than all the technical feats that Blair and his colleagues could accomplish? It was impossible.

But David Blair made his mark in British ballet. He was the male star of Britain's first full-length ballet, Cranko's three-act *The Prince of the Pagodas* (1957), and of Ashton's wholly new version of *La Fille Mal Gardée* (1960) in which he excelled in the great role of Colas, the hero of

traditional ballet's irresistible romantic comedy. There were Albrechts and Siegfrieds and Prince Florimunds also, but they were admirable without being distinctive or gripping. And so the career of David Blair as a dancer was blighted. He was, briefly, England's *premier danseur*, but whether he would ever have achieved international stardom if Nureyev had not come along is impossible to say. It was not easy to follow the handsome, dapper, warm, and much-loved Somes, and it was impossible to rival Nureyev. David Blair was a part, and a very fine part, of the male dance evolution of British ballet in a transitional period. He died young. He was only forty-three.

A contemporary of Blair's, John Gilpin, performed only infrequently, and then as guest artist, with Britain's Royal Ballet, but he brought great distinction to British ballet itself as a principal dancer with England's Ballet Rambert, Britain's oldest ballet company; with the London Festival Ballet, where he came under the influence of and enjoyed the coaching and guidance of Dolin; and through guest appearances with Roland Petit's Ballets de Paris, the American Ballet Theatre, and other companies around the world. Described as "a brilliant and noble dancer," he brought the elegance and poetic grace of a pure *danseur noble* to princely roles in *Giselle*, *Swan Lake*, and *The Sleeping Beauty*, and remarkable virtuosity to such bravura *pas de deux* as "The Bluebird," the "Peasant" *pas de deux* from *Giselle*, *Esmeralda*, and combined virtuosity with delicate lyricism in *Le Spectre de la Rose*.

In 1957, at twenty-seven, Gilpin appeared to be at the peak of his powers, physically still young but with more than a dozen years experience as a star dancer in a wide variety of roles in a number of companies, each with different styles and repertories. He was described as "a young Greek god" with a "perfectly proportioned" body, "astonishing elevation," and "superb physical control." Cyril Swinson, the dance writer, praised his "compelling stage personality" and "star quality" but went on to say that his was not "a strongly masculine personality, but warm and generous

Apollo with Henning Kronstam.

Henning Kronstam with Kirsten Simone
in Ashton's *Romeo and Juliet*.
Von Haven, Copenhagen

with an engaging *joie de vivre* and a charm of
elfin magic. This somewhat lightweight personality is at a disadvantage in those parts which
demand acting ability. Although he can fulfill superbly the technical requirement of the male
roles in classical ballets, his acting lacks the con-
viction that Dolin and Somes, Skibine, Youskevitch, Erik Bruhn, Fadeyechev, and others bring
to these parts."

Yet Gilpin had been a successful child actor.

At thirteen he had won the coveted Adeline
Genée Gold Medal by completing with honors
all of the Royal Academy of Dancing examinations and in 1957 he won the Prix Vaslav Nijinsky for his dancing in *Giselle* and other ballets
in Paris. Injuries and illnesses brought on an early
retirement, but not before he had brought honor
to British ballet and distinction to the art of the
male dancer.

The mantle of male ballet greatness, English
cut, worn with flourish by Dolin, with aristocratic
demeanor by Helpmann, noble grace by Somes,
has fallen on the princely shoulders of Anthony
Dowell. Here is that rare creature, the *premier*

87

danseur noble. Bruhn was one; Ivan Nagy, Hungarian-born, is one for America; Anthony Dowell is England's only *premier danseur noble* today, but one respected, admired, and royally cheered around the world. It has been said that a male dancer cannot learn to be a *premier danseur noble*, that whatever class he may have been born into physically, he is a born aristocrat of the dance. Dowell is that. There is a touch of *hauteur* about him. When he was very young, he was a trifle too haughty, too cool. But the underlying humor appeared and with it came graciousness and a touch of warmth. This air, rarefied but oh so pure and refreshing, is coupled with a lovely dancer's body: lean, long-limbed, lithe, topped by a handsome head. The dancing style is impeccably attuned to the style of the ballet at hand and the technique, seemingly effortless, is prodigious. And just at the instant that the viewer thinks he finds a quality of smugness or self-satisfaction or regal condescension in Dowell, a boyish smile dispels all such nonsense.

There is, however, a quality of remoteness about Anthony Dowell. He says of himself: "I tend to have a 'keep away' aura. There is a sort of glass box that falls around me and I seem to dare people to enter." But Dowell adds that he feels a new warmth has entered his performing: "I think of what just a single performance may do for someone—it's a lovely feeling! I think with me it has been the process of growing up."

At the start, there was no particular interest in dancing. "I went to the same school as my sister," says Dowell. "I showed no objections as a child. But what really gave me the bug were the class exams. They were held in a theater! The glitter! The backstage! It was 'theater,' not dance, that got to me. I might just as well have become an actor."

But at ten, in 1953, little Anthony commenced his studies at the Royal Ballet School and at seventeen, while still a student, became a member of the Covent Garden Opera Ballet. It was a short step to the Royal Ballet itself. It was made in 1962 and a featured part was given him the same year that Erik Bruhn cast him in the swift, soaring, virtuosic *pas de six* from Bournonville's *Napoli,* staged by Bruhn for the Royal.

Almost from the start, he has been an inspiration to choreographers, and for him they have designed a diversity of roles that have explored and exposed his potential and his versatility. Ashton, in 1964, created *The Dream,* a one-act, all-encompassing version of Shakespeare's *A Midsummer Night's Dream.* The leading male role, Oberon, was tailored for Anthony. Here was an aristocrat, a prince, in fact a young king. But he was to be unreal, a fairy (not a fairy-tale) king. So he moved with mercurial speed and incredible lightness. He was here; he was there; he was gone. He was visible and, as if you sensed only his aura, invisible. There was a boyish petulance about him when he couldn't have his own way and an almost childish glee in his plotted revenges against his fairy queen, Titania. And with it all, demands for technical displays that would terrify the average *danseur.* Not Anthony. He met all demands with aplomb and . . . amusement.

As he has matured in the part, he has had Oberon grow older too, not so much in years as in behavior. Dancing the role today, he seems almost to make a personal comment on the entire fanciful proceedings, rather like a glorious Shakespeare "aside," delivered kinetically.

The boyishness inherent in Dowell's appearance and that secret, "glassed-in" inner depth that he admits to were brilliantly fused by Antony Tudor in a ballet created especially for Anthony, *Shadowplay.* The central role of the jungle boy, resembling somewhat Kipling's Mowgli, requires an accomplished actor, as do most Tudor roles. In fact, it is more acting than it is bravura dancing; hence, it is not as much a favorite with the public at large as are those ballets allowing the *premier danseur* to be the athlete. Yet there is immense visceral power to the part of The Boy with the Matted Hair, as this young lord of the jungle is described, and there is the intensity of an ever-alert presence. The boy is, in truth, prepared to spring, to flee, to attack, to elude, as are the catlike beasts of the jungle, and so it is that one experiences tense anticipations while watching the youth in his shadowplay.

For is it a real jungle; or is it the jungle of the adolescent world? Dowell makes you aware of both in *Shadowplay* as he establishes, and re-

Niels Kehlet in the Royal Danish
Ballet's *Far from Denmark.*
John R. Johnsen, Copenhagen

turns, again and again, to a movement pattern in
which he assumes a semi-kneeling position, one
arm draped over the raised knee, as if he were sitting on an invisible throne or, better yet, en-
compassing the authority of the throne in his
very body, a mobile throne that must be free to
escape danger but ever present to assert authority
over place, creatures, man, self.

In Ashton's *Monotones,* all is cool and Dowell
dances with the authority and precision of a
Euclid stating a geometric process. In contrast is

his Romeo in MacMillan's *Romeo and Juliet,*
and if he is dancing with Antoinette Sibley, perhaps his ideal partner, the dimension of the poet
appears in his performing.

"I give myself to the choreographer," he says.
To the ballet coach, "Okay, but only if it feels
right to me." When he started his dancing career
he concentrated upon "doing the steps as correctly as possible." With *Shadowplay,* Tudor led
him into a wholly new concept of performing:
"This was the first ballet to have me really *think*
on stage—it was a breakthrough for me—how to
react to happenings and feelings, how to come
alive on stage." From there he learned "not to let
a performance drop after I've made a mistake; to

Niels Kehlet of the Royal Danish Ballet in a series of jumps from Bournonville's *Tyrolean Dance Variations* with Solveig Østergaard as the ballerina.

Frank Derbas

avoid being busy and agitated and look for economy of movement; to find and let your individual trademark come through. You accept what you have and enjoy it!"

Of his teachers and coaches, he feels that Somes did the most for him when he was learning the great classical roles. "He's fantastic! At the very first, of course, he expected me to be like him, but soon he led me to find myself. And I did just that." But self-discovery does not mean an end to learning. "I found the need for freezing one's movement in space by watching Ashton with Margot. There was a movement that didn't seem to project. Then Ashton had her hold a movement for just a fraction longer. The impact was terrific. I learned then that the dancer must *hold* a line so that it can register with an audience at a distance."

For Dowell, there is no recurring ecstasy in dancing. "I never fail to take one class a day— that makes it possible for you to lose your worries. Then, on stage I am mostly conscious of hoping that things will go well. If it happens that you are above such thoughts, it is a special dividend. So when performances work completely in every way, the experience is great!" Those moments, the daily class, the discipline of dance serve him as a person. "During bad times, dance took me through it." In 1976, an injury almost ended his career. I met him in the lobby of the Royal Opera House, Covent Garden, and he told me of the seriousness of his injury. "I have one last hope for treatment in Denmark and if that doesn't work . . ." He shrugged and then smiled. "If it doesn't maybe I'll have to become the actor we talked about last year."

Happily, Anthony Dowell recovered and returned to dance brilliantly at the peak of his powers. But he knows that one day, injuries to one side, he will no longer be able to dance the traditional classics and the stellar roles created especially for him by master choreographers. When virtuosity is gone, what will he do? "I'm spoiled," he says. "I don't want ever to do lesser roles. I think I would return to my first love, designing for the stage.

"But if a director-producer came along and believed in me, in my potential as an actor, I'd jump at it. I need the spotlight and I'll follow any path that will keep me in its glow."

* * *

DENMARK is the oldest kingdom in Europe. Not surprisingly, the Kingdom of Denmark boasts the oldest, unbroken ballet tradition in Europe. There were court ballets in Copenhagen as far back as 1559, even before the milestone *Ballet Comique de la Reine* was presented in Paris (1581). Professional ballet came to the stage in Denmark as early as 1722, and in 1748 the Royal Dancers were a major component of the Royal Theater. Regular ballet instruction began in the 1750s, and in 1771 the Royal Ballet School was formally established under the direction of a French ballet master, Pierre Laurent. But the fame of Danish Ballet rests primarily with the great nineteenth-century Danish choreographer August Bournonville. His ballets formed the backbone of Danish repertory throughout the century and remain in this century as the pride of Denmark and the envy of other ballet theaters. August was the son of Antoine Bournonville, a French dancer, pupil of Noverre and the *premier danseur* for King Gustav III of Sweden, before coming to Copenhagen as a principal dancer. The son, August Bournonville, not only studied with his Noverre-trained father, with the Italian choreographer Vincenzo Galeotti, director and chief choreographer of the Royal Danish Ballet, but also in Paris with Auguste Vestris.

Bournonville's studies in Paris took place during the years 1820–28. These are of utmost significance to ballet, for this was a transitional period linking two great eras of ballet. From Vestris, the greatest male dancer of his day, he learned all there was to know about the classical dance for men to date. He learned the style of classical French dance and the technique and years later he put these, in capsule, into his ballet *Konservatoriet* (The Conservatory) of 1849. This is the best surviving record of the French school of classical dancing. But Bournonville was in Paris when the female dancer was beginning to use *pointe*, although she could do little more

Peter Martins at the age of eleven,
in 1958, in the Bournonville class
at the Royal Theater in Copenhagen.
Ralph McWilliams

than stand or step briefly onto toe, and when, with this invention, the classical ballets of royal court-origins, with themes of Greek gods and heroes, disappeared, the Romantic Age of Ballet was born.

August Bournonville, knowledgeable heir to past ballet accomplishments, an active participant in the new styles and techniques of a new ballet age and a male dancer who had no intention of downgrading the male dancer while the ballerina was rising onto *pointe*, became a unique

choreographer for his time and for his posterity. When Paris and the rest of Europe were dismissing the *danseur* as expendable, Copenhagen was maintaining equal rights for men in ballet and even, in some instances, giving the male the edge over the female. As a dancer, Bournonville himself was especially skilled in *batterie*, in steps of elevation, usually the special province of the male. Thus, instead of electing to have the male support the ballerina on her newly discovered, perilous *pointe*, he required the ladies to leap, jump, and beat along with the gentlemen. So when the male dancer in ballet was going to hell everywhere else, he flourished in Denmark without a break down to the very present, with the Bournonville School of the Royal Theater producing not only girls who are aerialists but also men who are in the front ranks of the great male dancers of the century.

Bournonville's most celebrated male pupil, and his successor as ballet master, was Hans Beck, a brilliant *premier danseur* in the Vestris-Bournonville style. He lived for ninety-one years and it was chiefly his devotion to Bournonville

Peter Martins in *The Nutcracker*,
the New York City Ballet.
Martha Swope

that kept alive the Bournonville ballets and saw the establishment of a training system of six classes (one for every day of the week except Sunday) incorporating the chief ingredients of Bournonville style, steps, *enchaînements*. Bournonville had ruled Danish ballet, with a few interruptions, from 1828 until his death in 1879, and Beck, born in 1861, once his long dancing career was over and his tenure as director had ended, continued to coach Bournonville ballets and keep a sharp eye on the style and technique of the boys of the Royal Danish Ballet until his death in 1952.

Beck dedicated his dance life to Denmark alone. His successor as *premier danseur*, Børge Ralov, was a brilliant dancer but he too elected to serve ballet at home rather than abroad. Actually, the title *premier danseur* had never been formally bestowed on any Danish male dancer until Ralov was so named, for the Royal Danish Ballet traditionally has divided its members into two groups, *balletdancers* and *solodancers*.

Ralov was barely seen by audiences outside of Denmark, for he retired from the stage just four years after the Royal Danish Ballet ventured outside the kingdom in 1953 for its first triumphal appearances in London. But balletomanes from around the world, drawn to Copenhagen after World War II by the unique Bournonville ballets, not only were captivated by the company but also praised and prized the dancing of Ralov.

But the first Danish male dancer to achieve international fame was Erik Bruhn. Erik, a true *danseur noble* of princely presence, was a hero off stage as well as on. As a pupil at the Royal Ballet School in Copenhagen during the German occupation of World War II, little Erik was a courier for the Danish underground. He, along with other student dancers such as Fredbjørn Bjørnsson, going to and from school were able to deliver messages important to Denmark's intensely patriotic and almost universal resistance movement against the Nazis. Erik, born in 1928, entered the Royal School by audition (as do all children of the Royal Theater schools) in 1937. Ten years later, having passed his difficult final examinations as an aspirant, he was accepted into the company itself in which, like other students, he had performed as a child dancer while a student. The same year he made his first guest appearance outside Denmark and two years later, in 1949, when he was promoted to soloist rank, he joined the American Ballet Theatre for two years.

Peter Martins with Suzanne Farrell in Bournonville's *Divertissements*, New York City Ballet.
Martha Swope

I well remember Erik's first seasons with the American company. He was very young, very blond, very handsome, very well schooled, very neat, and . . . very bland. Promising, even admirable, but not terribly exciting. In 1951 he returned to Denmark—throughout his dancing career he has had permission to appear abroad for long periods of time while retaining his post and privileges with the Royal Danish Ballet—and came under the tutelage of one of the great ballet teachers of the century, Vera Volkova, just appointed principal teacher—and later artistic advisor—to the Royal Danish Ballet. Bruhn, trained almost exclusively in Bournonville style before leaving Denmark, found in Volkova a brilliant coach. In terms of pedagogical descent, Mme. Volkova was a pupil and a favorite of Agrippina Vaganova, the greatest teacher in the Soviet Union and one who gave her name to a way of teaching, the Vaganova Method. Her center was Leningrad and her theater the Kirov (formerly the Maryinsky). And the ballet school for the Maryinsky was molded on the teaching of its principal pedagogue for forty years (1860–1903), Christian Johansson, a pupil of Denmark's Bournonville.

Thus it was that Volkova brought to Denmark, long shut off balletically from the rest of the world and its dance developments, the most advanced technical training possible, but with an ancient heritage stemming back to Bournonville himself. Erik was trained and guided by this vivid, intense, immensely gifted woman who also guided on the road to greatness such ballerinas as England's Margot Fonteyn and America's Maria Tallchief.

Erik's return to the American Ballet Theatre in 1955 seemed, on the surface, to be merely routine: the re-engagement of a young soloist following a tour of ballet duty in his homeland. But such was not the case. ABT's tour opened in Princeton, New Jersey. Erik was scheduled to dance the "Black Swan" *pas de deux* with the company's prima ballerina, Nora Kaye. It was always a surefire assignment for Kaye since she was a strong technician, her balances were superb, and she always executed the thirty-two *fouettés* of the coda more perfectly than almost any of her colleagues, never moving off a place barely larger than a dime while a-spin. It seemed, in advance, the usual thing—a ballerina in a *tour de force* accompanied by a gracious, helpful cavalier. Such was not to be the case. Kaye was superb but the bland blond boy had developed fire and pulsating impact. He had become too a virtuoso, a star. The house went mad. Miss Kaye, happy for him and irreverent about herself, was heard to mutter as she left the stage, "Well, get that kid! Mother had better get her tail moving!"

For the next dozen years, Erik reigned supreme as the world's greatest *premier danseur noble*. There were, of course, other great dancers, the spectacular Vladimir Vasiliev from the Soviet Union and America's brilliant Edward Villella among them, but Bruhn, in his dancing, combined an almost lofty elegance with the sheer physical prowess of an Olympic athlete. He did not execute and exploit the hazards of difficult dance steps; he surmounted them. I remember seeing him, on the rustic stage of the Ted Shawn Theater at the Jacob's Pillow Dance Festival, unreeling *tours à la seconde* from which he would rise to the highest of half toe and spin on momentum alone for five revolutions. The audience gasped but Erik presented this incredible *étude* in suspension with the same ease he brought to a *grand révérence*, the courtly bow to his partner. For the twentieth century, he was the consummate aristocrat, the king of dancers.

But with this aristocracy, with this regal surmounting of technical demands, there was no longer any blandness, no sense of withdrawal. Lean, slight, very fair, and with an air of gentlemanly delicacy (not delicateness) about him, he nevertheless came over with impact. He did not so much project in the vaudevillian sense as he *drew* audiences to him, rather like a magnet. He was, of course, the perfect ballet prince, the aris-tocrat; a cheered and lauded matinee with the then greatest Giselle of the day, Alicia Markova, not only placed him in the position of America's foremost Albrecht but also America's foremost *danseur noble*. Naturally, in the Bournonville repertory, he became the definitive James, the Scottish hero, in *La Sylphide* as far as the American public was concerned, though he was equaled and possibly bettered by the Royal Dane who headed the Royal Danish Ballet at home, Henning Kronstam.

As his career expanded, Bruhn added intensely dramatic and sensual roles to his repertory. He had, of course, communicated that restrained ardor necessary to the romantic classics, but in such ballets as Roland Petit's *Carmen* and Birgit Cullberg's *Miss Julie*, an almost violent passion was produced along with a sexuality that would have been described in the vernacular as close to "dirty." Petit, of course, had been a brilliant, smoldering, oversexed Don José in his own *Carmen*, but Erik in a jet-black wig was his match as the male voluptuary. When he danced with the Royal Danish Ballet, who performed the best *Carmen* to be found since the initial days with Petit's Ballets de Paris and Jeanmaire as Carmen, the very blond ballerina Kirsten Simone, also in black wig, was his Carmen. And so sexy were these Scandinavians in dark Latin roles that balletomanes used to say that at last they had discovered a torrid nature lurking beneath the cool and fair Danish exterior. Certainly they discovered it in Erik, and the unsuspected quality opened up new areas of performing for him.

Bruhn, of course, danced with many ballerinas: Nora Kaye, the senior Markova in *Giselle*—his partnering was fabled—Simone, and especially Maria Tallchief. Although their partnership did not span a long period of time and although it was interrupted by assignments separating them, Bruhn and Tallchief were in fact briefly "a team." With the American Ballet Theatre they made a particularly forceful duo, in Europe as well as in America, with their sizzling performance in *Miss Julie* in which the love-eager, aristocratic heroine seduces her butler. There might have been a further successful partnership within the framework of the New York City Ballet but

Balanchine's increasing distaste for stars and his even greater dislike of "teams" nipped the potential partnership of Tallchief-Bruhn before it had had a chance to flower in the Balanchine repertory. Because of this Balanchine aversion, Bruhn did not remain with the company long and Tallchief, its first great ballerina, finally left when she stated to the press that she was not only being listed alphabetically, she was "being treated alphabetically." Bruhn, during his frequent associations with ABT, also performed to special acclaim in partnership with that brilliant virtuosa Lupe Serrano.

When Bruhn chose to retire, at forty, from those virtuoso assignments that had brought him world renown, he did it because he never wanted the public to have to say, "I remember when he used to . . ." Slowly he turned to parts with which he had not been associated in the past and with new roles created for him. Instead of dancing James in *La Sylphide*, he put putty on his face, deep lines, gray hair, a stooped back, and

malevolent eye and mimed the key role of Madge, the witch. As an actor, and actor-dancer, a restager of the classics, an original choreographer, and a ballet director, Bruhn has experienced total theater, but for the world of ballet he will always be remembered and recorded as a dancer, the greatest *danseur noble* of his time.

As for himself, Bruhn says, "I love dancing and I want to go on dancing for the rest of my life." In the spring-summer of 1978, he found a way. With the Fort Worth Ballet, he essayed a whole new style of dance by performing the title role in a rock ballet, *Rasputin—The Holy Devil*, choreographed by James Clouser. The onetime *premier danseur noble* did not feel out of his element in modern movements to rock music: "I feel perfectly natural in these movements and the style doesn't seem like alien territory." From there, he moved into the repertory of the late modern dance star, José Limón—he had already danced Limón's *The Moor's Pavane* as produced by ballet companies, but now he was dancing the

97

role of Othello in an all-modern dance troupe, the José Limón Dance Company, where he mastered other Limón roles, some that had been performed when Limón was past sixty. The "maturity" of roles in modern dance repertory has convinced Bruhn that although the Albrechts and Siegfrieds are behind him, he can indeed go on dancing "for the rest of my life."

Another great Dane, Henning Kronstam, also belongs in the *danseur noble* category and, like Bruhn, he is also a brilliant actor-dancer. He was the first of the great Danish male dancers to be almost wholly Volkova-trained. Of course, as with all the boys at the Royal School, Bournonville classes were mandatory and Kronstam grew into a superb exponent of Bournonville, but because of his Volkova instruction in the advanced techniques of the day and through her remarkable coaching, Kronstam became a brilliant executant and interpreter of all of ballet's classics, *Swan Lake*, *The Sleeping Beauty*, *Giselle*, *Coppélia*, *La Sylphide*, *Les Sylphides*, and the various *grands pas de deux*.

All of the Bournonville ballets, in addition to *La Sylphide*, have been enhanced by Kronstam's performances, for Henning, along with all of the dancers of the Royal Danish Ballet, are excellent actors. This acting is not by any means exclusively the traditional mime of the old Coralli and later Petipa ballets, for even when the Danes follow the traditional mime lines, they imbue them with a gestural contemporaneity and with an individual stress or accent that make them seem personal as well as immediate.

But aside from the inherited Bournonville and Petipa roles, Henning created new parts and achieved a brilliant identity in certain non-Danish contemporary ballets entering the Royal repertory. In the latter category, it should be noted that Henning was very possibly the best Poet ever to act and partner in Balanchine's *La Sonnambula* (also, *Night Shadow*), equaled only by Frederic Franklin, and that his Iago, in Limón's *The Moor's Pavane*, could send chills down the viewer's back.

Of the new and major creations for the Royal Danish Ballet, none was more prestigious than Frederick Ashton's *Romeo and Juliet* (to the Prokofiev score) produced in 1955 and starring Mona Vangsaae as Juliet and Kronstam as Romeo. This was the first full-length Prokofiev *Romeo* to be produced outside of the Soviet Union and its success was nothing short of sensational, not only in Copenhagen but also at New York's Metropolitan Opera House, where enthusiasm ran so high that S. Hurok, the great impresario, moaned, "If I had only known, I would have booked this *Romeo* for a Broadway run!" Vangsaae was a beautiful and vulnerable Juliet, but it was Henning, unbelievably handsome, young (twenty), and passionate that had audiences screaming.

Henning has made guest appearances with companies outside Denmark, and most successfully, but he has concentrated his career in his homeland and moved from the *danseur* roles, the virtuoso assignments, to *demi-caractère* parts, to mime characterizations and, in 1977, to appointment as director of the Royal Danish Ballet. Rather melancholy, or at least serious, off stage and rather shy and moody, Henning has always excelled in comedy. This unsuspected quality emerged with impact when he danced the small, secondary role of the Toreador in Petit's *Carmen* and gave it such caricatured vanity that he came close to taking the honors away from Bruhn and Simone. Tragicomedy was also a forte, as in Petit's ballet of *Cyrano de Bergerac*, and the crystal purity and godly radiance of Balanchine's *Apollo* were his in full measure.

Looking back at the Henning Kronstam of the 1950s and 1960s, the balletomane may well wonder if Kronstam could have become an international superstar of ballet. He appeared to have every quality and qualification for such a rank if he had elected to join an international company outside of Denmark. But perhaps he was always meant to be a very special jewel among the resplendent ballet stars produced over the years in the Kingdom of Denmark.

Fredbjørn Bjørnsson was never a *premier danseur noble*, never a first-rank exponent of Petipa or Balanchine, but he was, and is, one of the great dancers of our time. Small, black-haired, with large expressive eyes and a mouth in which lurks the promise of a mischievous smile, Freddie communicated the zest and fun of living. In the Royal Danish Ballet's staging of *Coppélia* (by Hans Beck in 1896), Freddie was the great Franz of his era as a virtuoso character dancer (1950s and into the '60s). The leaps were soaring, the czardas ebullient, and the characterization of the ardent, daring, thoughtless hero was brilliant. And what has been especially notable is that when it came time for him to pass the role of Franz on to a Danish successor, he took over the role of the old toymaker, Dr. Coppélius, and created a portrayal, touching as well as funny, deeply human as well as amusingly irascible, that has no equal.

His performance of the title role in Fokine's *Petrouchka* belongs in the company of that handful of artists, beginning with Nijinsky, who have succeeded in finding the essence of the puppet with the feelings of a human. But fans on both sides of the Atlantic almost always think of Freddie Bjørnsson as the supreme Bournonville dancer, the dashing hero of *Napoli*, the flying Scottish dancer in Act I of *La Sylphide* in that dazzling solo now usually danced by the hero, James, and the bounding *danseur* in such favorite *pas de deux* as those from *Flower Festival in Genzano* and *Kermesse in Bruges*, duets that are to the Bournonville repertory what the "Black Swan" and "Don Quixote" *pas de deux* are to Petipa virtuosi.

Freddie was a special favorite of the late King Frederik IX of Denmark. It began on a Danish beach when a very tall young gentleman tousled the hair of little Freddie as he dashed by kicking up sand and said, "What is your name?" The lad replied, "Freddie. What's yours?" The tall man looked down and smiled. "My name's Fred too." It was the Crown Prince of Denmark. Many years later, when Fredbjørn was first presented to the King in the royal box in the Royal Theater following a command performance, he bowed low and said, "Your Majesty." The King smiled as Bjørnsson looked up. "Oh, have you forgotten? Just call me Fred!" The very democratic King was given to telephoning his subjects if he wanted to say something directly without going

through royal protocol. Once the Bjørnsson phone rang early in the morning while Freddie was shaving. His son answered and called, "It's for you, Dad." "Tell whoever it is to wait while I finish shaving." Then when Freddie finally answered, the deep voice said, "Here is the King." Freddie, with lather on his face, fell to his knees and moaned, "Majesty!" The King, an ardent devotee of Bournonville ballet and himself an expert musician, simply asked: "Mr. Bjørnsson, I was curious as to why, last evening in the last act of *Napoli*, you tossed your hat stage right on the first beat of the measure instead of on the third as you usually do—and as the score might indicate?" His Majesty knew his Bournonville, his ballet music, and particularly the phrasing of one of his royal dancers, the one male dancer he admired the most and whom he knighted in 1961.

Niels Kehlet, a brilliant product of the great Volkova, oddly enough is a logical successor to Bjørnsson in those *demi-caractère* roles, found especially in Bournonville, demanding absolutely first-rank technique along with a command of detailed characterization. Kehlet is, perhaps, a trifle too small and his face too cherubic (or impish, depending on the mood) for Albrechts, Siegfrieds, and assorted Prince Charmings, but he is a superb Franz in *Coppélia* and, because of his elevation, *ballon*, brilliant *batterie*, and superb musical phrasing, he is a natural for all Bournonville's athletic, boyish, comedic, virtuosic, dramatic male roles. In abstract ballets, such as Harald Lander's *Etudes*, that fantastic choreographic celebration of the ballet dancer's training, discipline, prowess, and crowning elegance of action, Kehlet is outstanding. In Fokine's *Le Spectre de la Rose*, the boyishness, the impishness, the athleticism disappear and he becomes a creature, a figment of dreams. It is not just that his performance is as technically flawless as a human could achieve but, rather, that magically he makes you see the rose spirit through the eyes of the sleeping, dreaming girl. It is evanescence made indelible.

Kehlet is a master of contemporary ballets as well as of the Bournonville and Fokine classics. His Evil Magician in Birgit Cullberg's Lapland fantasy, *Moon Reindeer*, fairly trembles with sor-

cery whether he is crouching in wait for his prey or soaring like a vulture, talons bared, for the capture. The Russian Petipa is not beyond his style if the roles are right: the Jester in *Swan Lake* (a part not seen often outside Russia or Denmark) becomes an essential, not an addendum, in his care and, of course, his Bluebird in *The Sleeping Beauty* is a model of Petipa style. One can almost predict that Kehlet like Bjørnsson, when the time comes, will promote himself to the great acting

roles of Danish, and world, ballets, for time seems to hold no terror for the remarkable actors-dancers of the Kingdom of Denmark.

Denmark is a small country, a little over four million people live there, yet it has produced one of the world's great ballet companies and many of the world's finest dancers, especially among the men. Bournonville danced in Paris; Beck stayed home. Bruhn danced with companies around the

Peter Schaufuss in a classical movement.
Martha Swope

Peter Schaufuss in a dancing pose.
Jack Mitchell

world and became a global *premier danseur absolute*; Bjørnsson and Kehlet, though guesting in Europe, were primarily associated with their home company. Kronstam, guest artist in both America and Europe, essentially headed the Royal Danish Ballet as its undisputed classical dance star. But later male Danes have nearly, but not quite, severed ties (if not ties, duties) with their Danish colleagues, if not their Danish heritage. Both Peter Martins and Peter Schaufuss, products of the Royal School and of the Royal Danish Ballet, are now international stars with their roots firmly planted in the New World. Helgi Tomasson, an Icelander, was taught by Volkova as his principal mentor and by Bruhn, whose protégé he was. For a time, he served as a dancer at the famed Pantomime Theater in Copenhagen's celebrated Tivoli Gardens.

Tomasson is almost a dancer's dancer, that is,

his cleanness of balletic line, his accuracy of step, his exact musical phrasing, the retention of unadorned classical schooling are qualities that dancers seek to attain and hence look for in others. Many of the technical niceties they relish are lost on the general public or simply accepted as "routine." Thus it is that Helgi comes across quietly and attractively but with no flamboyance, no highly personal idiosyncrasies to make him a . . . personality. Nureyev can stand absolutely still on stage and all eyes are riveted upon him; Bruhn could do the same; with Helgi, you grade him on the extent of his doing. It is ever a joy to watch Helgi Tomasson, for he comes close to being impeccable, but it is rarely a thrill.

With Peter Schaufuss, it is a thrill. The impeccable technique is there, but with it comes a physical virtuosity that is not very far removed

Peter Schaufuss in Act III of *Swan Lake*.
Linda Vartoogian

from that of Mikhail Baryshnikov. The budding actor is present too, a cavalier who can be passionate as well as princely, impetuous as well as imperious. But one expects acting accomplishments from a graduate of the Royal Danish

Ballet. Peter's dance heritage, however, goes even deeper. His father, Frank Schaufuss, was a vivid actor-dancer with the Royal Danish Ballet—his was a fine Mercutio as was Bjørnsson's in Ashton's *Romeo and Juliet*—and briefly director of the Royal Dancers; and his mother, Mona Vangsaae was not only a glorious Juliet but the first of the Bournonville-trained dancers to excel in the new, abstract ballets of Balanchine.

Peter Schaufuss, like Tomasson, became a regular member of the New York City Ballet but, as had been the case with Bruhn years before, his tenure was brief. The reason? He was independent by nature and, because he had both the talent and the temperament, he knew that he could become a ballet superstar as did Bruhn. This is not the image of a Balanchine performer, but even more important, Schaufuss wanted, as had Bruhn, to make his mark in the great classics of Petipa, Fokine, Bournonville and these are not (with the exception of Bournonville *Divertissements*) part of the repertory of the New York City Ballet. Peter Schaufuss had to go elsewhere. He went to the National Ballet of Canada, under the new direction of Alexander Grant in 1977, and in New York performances in *Giselle* and *Swan Lake* at the Metropolitan Opera House, he became an overnight sensation. He had been dancing right next door at the New York State Theater with the New York City Ballet and he had been admired but he had needed the showcase of a lavishly produced, narrative-ballet classic filled with flights of virtuosity, intense romance, and violent drama to become a star. Naturally, he was not invited back to the Balanchine company, so he became *premier danseur* of Canada's National Ballet, thus culminating his earlier stints with London's Festival Ballet and guest performances with the San Francisco Ballet and other troupes and, of course, the invaluable if ephemeral exposure to the genius of Balanchine.

Years ago, I baby-sat for Peter in Copenhagen along with his father, Frank, one evening when Mona was dancing. I don't believe that then either Frank or Mona thought of a dance career for their son or, if they did, that he would become one of the most exciting dancers Denmark had produced in the twentieth century. I had had no such doubts about another Peter, Peter Martins, when I had first seen him as that attractive child-student in a Bournonville class.

The adult Martins, tall, blond, big but light and lithe, is a dancer of the very top echelon in matters of virtuosity. His dramatic development, because of the very nature of Balanchine repertory in which the musical stimulus is paramount and the dramatic (or theatrical) element very minor, is not yet in full flower artistically. In his occasional appearances with his home company, one can see that acting skills and individualism, though latent, are present. But he is a great admirer of Balanchine, even a disciple, so he has not elected to make the great classical ballets a showcase for his talents. His Danish humor, his personal warmth, even a hint of bravura peek out in his initial attempts at choreography, which, though strongly influenced by Balanchine, are in no way slavish copies of the master.

But he has attained a quiet stardom within the framework of the starless New York City Ballet. Balanchine has created roles especially for him, among them the male lead in one of the masterpieces to emerge from the Stravinsky Festival produced by the NYCB in 1972, *Violin Concerto*. Jerome Robbins too has been inspired by both his handsome, virile presence and his musicality, creating for him the romantic *In the Night* (Chopin) and the monumental choreo-architectured *The Goldberg Variations* (Bach). He has been a frequent, successful, and popular partner of Suzanne Farrell, a Balanchine favorite who defected to Béjart, returned to the fold, and dances and behaves like a ballerina. They are *almost* a team but are not, naturally, exploited as such.

Peter Martins, in a direct line of descent through his Bournonville ancestry of Auguste Vestris, whose father, Gaetan, was hailed as the God of the Dance, is potentially an heir to that noble ballet title. For when he strides on stage with large-stepped grace and authority, he does indeed resemble a Golden God, a Viking deity-warrior rather than a French *dieu*; and one day, when he is a trifle older, he may throw that mantle of majesty about him, as Nureyev does with his cloak as Romeo or Albrecht or Siegfried, and take command of the stage. Peter has said that he is not interested in becoming a superstar, that being a dancer and a good one is all that he asks for; but I remember Bournonville looking down upon a ten-year-old from the ancient studio wall and I can hear the echo of my own voice: "That boy is going to be a star!"

10

SOME HONORED SOCIALIST-PEOPLES' ARTISTS AND SOME DAZZLING DEFECTORS

RUSSIAN BALLET did not leave Russia in 1909 with Serge Diaghilev, nor did Russian ballet come to an end with the Russian Revolution of 1917. True, the great male dancers and, in some cases, major choreographers were lost to the West—Nijinsky, Mordkin, Fokine, Massine, Lifar, Youskevitch, Eglevsky—along with a galaxy of great male teachers—Nicholas Legat, Oboukhoff, Vladimirov, Vilzak, and others—and a twentieth-century genius, George Balanchine. Still, Russian ballet under the Soviet regime not only continued but flourished. And mid-century, the Union of Soviet Socialist Republics and the United States of America began to produce some of the greatest male ballet dancers the world has ever seen. Why the U.S.S.R. and the U.S.A.? Perhaps one major link was the avid interest in athletics, in Olympics, in professional and amateur sports, in the prowess of the male.

The lowly status of the male ballet dancer in

(Overleaf) Yuri Soloviev in *Le Corsaire*.

the nineteenth century as manifested in Paris, the ballet capital of the world, and elsewhere did not leave Russia uninfected. Most of the male roles in the great Petipa-Ivanov classics, the backbone of classical ballet repertory to this day, were mime parts for the heroes, *porteurs* at best, or character parts that required character dancing. The Prince in *The Sleeping Beauty* as it was first produced did not dance, he partnered. Sometimes he passed on the duties of the partner to a younger, more agile dancer and reserved for himself assignments of acting and of presence.

There were, of course, the exceptions. In the latter half of the nineteenth century, Pavel Gerdt, Russian-born but of German heritage, became Russia's foremost *premier danseur*. Among

his teachers was the Bournonville-trained Johansson who had brought with him from his native Stockholm (where Antoine Bournonville had danced) and Copenhagen (where he had worked with August Bournonville) the skills, the stature, and the ever-challenging virtuosities of the Bournonville male dancer. Johansson, the story goes, never gave the same *enchaînement* twice during his long teaching career in St. Petersburg. Every combination for every class was newly conceived, ordered, and taught. It was, in fact, choreographed. For special pupils with special gifts, his *enchaînements* took in steps and sequences of steps that would exploit and challenge and train that particular dancer. Gerdt was a natural dancer but it was undoubtedly Johansson who made him the greatest Russian male dancer of the day.

Gerdt appeared in many of the Petipa-Ivanov ballets, in new stagings of the old Romantic Age ballets and, as time passed, gave greater accent to his acting skills and to that elegance of mien and deportment which made him the perfect *danseur noble*. At the peak of his career, he resented the custom that gave the *premier danseur* little dancing to do and was at his happiest when a role emerged that took equal parts of dancing and acting to make the whole.

Gerdt in turn taught Vassily Tikhomirov who became the great male star for the closing decade of the last century and for two decades into this (he died in 1956). Tikhomirov, Moscow-trained and situated, was sent to St. Petersburg, as were many of the exceptionally gifted dancers, for polishing at the Imperial School in the Imperial capital. Here he too worked with Christian Johansson and gained a reputation for exuberant leaps and dashing virility characteristic of the Bournonville style. This, in time, became the Moscow style for the male dancer: big, heroic, valiant. And Tikhomirov applied this not only to the old classics but also the new ballets by Gorsky and others. But although active and honored after the Revolution, he fought for the retention of the classics even during a difficult period when socialist propaganda ballets all but eliminated the fairy-tale masterpieces of the past.

Complete products of the Soviet regime were

Alexei Yermolayev, who did not begin his Leningrad studies until he was fourteen, and Vakhtang Chaboukiani (from Tbilisi in Georgia), who was sixteen when he was permitted to enter classes for "overage" but talented applicants at the state school in Leningrad. Both achieved remarkable virtuosity and both advanced the stature of the male dancer in the Soviet Union. But it was Chaboukiani, twice winner of the Stalin Prize, Peoples' Artist of the U.S.S.R., who became the greatest male star of his day in the Soviet Union, the first Soviet ballet star to perform in the United States (1934), and the first Russian male dancer to achieve international recognition, at least in ballet circles, through Soviet ballet movies. In addition he was a choreographer who

achieved distinction not only through original ballets (*Laurencia* and *The Heart of the Hills*) but also by adapting some of the dances from the old classics to include passages that would give him opportunity to display his brilliant technique. These much-"altered" male variations are now performed by a legion of his successors at home and throughout the dancing world.

For those who never saw Chaboukiani in the flesh, a visit to a dance film library is very much in order. The movie technique, from the 1930s and 1940s, is dated, the costuming is sometimes silly, and the theatrics may amuse the viewer, but the powerful presence of Chaboukiani is there and so too are fragmentary examples of a virtuosity that will let you know—and no mistake about it—that you are watching one of the great male dancers of the ballet. For those outside the U.S.S.R. unfamiliar with a great number of Soviet-made ballets, Chaboukiani comes to them through choreography, adapted choreography, and especially interpretation in such familiar outlets for the male star as the *pas de deux* from *Le Corsaire, Don Quixote, The Flames of Paris*, for he is in all of them.

When the Bolshoi Ballet left Moscow for a season in London in 1956 and a debut in New York in 1959, audiences were impressed by massive settings and productions. Less appreciated were massive male dancers built roughly like American truck drivers. New Yorkers, justifiably, went wild over Galina Ulanova, the prima ballerina who had been fairly described as "The Wonder of the World," and by the volcanic Maya Plisetskaya. In the *demi-caractère* department there was some exciting male dancing, although not as stunning as that displayed by the ballet-trained folk dancers of the Moiseyev Dance Company from Moscow who had visited earlier. But in the major offering, Leonid Lavrovsky's historic choreography for the Serge Prokofiev *Romeo and Juliet*, the Romeo, Yuri Zhdanov, was as strong as a horse and totally lacking in the svelteness we had come to expect.

Vakhtang Chaboukiani in a scene from *The Flames of Paris*.

Zhdanov's heaviness was compounded by his attire in this and other ballets. Russian prudery had long insisted that the male wear underpants (instead of a brief, tight dance belt) under his tights and short pants over his tights. Often, the tunic had to come low enough to cover the entire pelvic area. All of this gave a thickness to the male body without indicating that size was due to muscles not to fat or flesh. In due course, the overpants were eliminated but under-drawers continued to be used except in the dress of the younger, or more defiant, male artists who were willing to be influenced by Western ballet dress.

However, first American audiences caught a glimpse of what was to become a new breed of Soviet male ballet stars in Vladimir Vasiliev. Just past his nineteenth birthday, he danced the role of Danila in *The Stone Flower* at New York's Metropolitan Opera House in 1959. Audiences leaned forward. Here was a young, slender, handsome Russian with presence, a romantic air, and technique. He was soon to become the golden-haired boy of the Bolshoi Ballet with audiences around the world, foreign tours, and at home a favorite with few if any equals. The air of romance was extended further when he married his classmate Yekaterina Maximova and became her regular partner, thus establishing, for the Bolshoi

Chaboukiani, probably in *Le Corsaire*.

Chaboukiani in *Elf*.

Ballet and for balletomanes outside of Russia, a "team" in the manner of Markova-Dolin, Fonteyn-Nureyev, and the like.

Vasiliev is not only the Bolshoi Ballet's *premier danseur*, he is a true product of the Bolshoi School, yet with a difference. Following the Revolution, when the capital was moved from Leningrad, every effort was made to assure the ascendancy of Moscow in all matters, ballet included. Although the Vaganova Choreographic Institute (earlier the Leningrad Ballet School) trained superb dancers, Ulanova among them, very often the best were moved to Moscow and the Bolshoi. Yuri Grigorovich, artistic director of the Bolshoi Ballet, was Leningrad-trained but has gained his

Classes for the Bolshoi Ballet.

fame as a choreographer for the Bolshoi. In 1977 he told me that he felt that Soviet ballet had entered a new era in which the best of the two schools—Kirov and Bolshoi—had become, or were becoming, fused.

Grigorovich said that the vitality and warmth of the Moscow style were not incompatible with the cool lyricism and the elegance of the Kirov School and that he himself as both director and principal choreographer was working toward this goal. In casting his ballets, he has frequently given Vasiliev opportunities not only to display his personal talents but to proclaim that very fusion of styles. For Vasiliev, lean and handsome, has the bearing of the *premier danseur*, the ele-

gant line of the prince in ballet, yet there is present in him the strength to exude dramatic violence when called for and unabashed bravura in technical feats. He is an aristocratic cavalier in *The Sleeping Beauty* or in *The Nutcracker* (both in new versions by Grigorovich), but in the new *Ivan the Terrible* (by Grigorovich), he becomes a barbaric king, fierce in love and fierce in political power struggles, and to Grigorovich's *Spartacus*, he manages to combine a tenderness and a heroic idealism with primitive thrusts of action.

Vasiliev's Leningrad counterpart was—he died, possibly a suicide, in 1977—Yuri Soloviev, *premier danseur* of the Kirov Ballet. The two, born the same year (1940), came to be the prime *premiers danseurs*, the first first-dancers, for their

particular generation in the Soviet Union. Soloviev, in the tradition of Nijinsky, was celebrated for his elevation, and he numbered among his most popular and spectacular assignments, the "Bluebird" variation in *The Sleeping Beauty*. He also danced the Prince in the same ballet, Siegfried in *Swan Lake*, and excelled in contemporary Soviet ballets, among them, the patriotic *Leningrad Symphony* (Belsky-Shostakovich), in which he created the role of the Youth. A feature-length movie of the complete Kirov Ballet's *The Sleeping Beauty* in which he dances the Prince records

Romeo and Juliet with
Yuri Zhdanov and Galina Ulanova.

forever Soloviev's superb dancing of classical ballet.

The three young Soviet contenders for positions of eminence in Soviet ballet are all associated with the Bolshoi. There is the big, blond, butch Alexander Godunov, Latvian-born, with powerful muscles, powerful technique, and a powerful presence. He has been a favored partner of the veteran Plisetskaya, dancing the role of Karenin in the ballerina's first full-length ballet, *Anna Karenina,* and partnering her in the passionate *La Rose Malade,* created especially for the Bolshoi's *prima ballerina assoluta* by France's Roland Petit. Godunov is a macho-type artist. He seems almost like a Westerner in speech (his English is good) and in dress (he would have qualified for a hippie a few years back). Moscow-born Vatcheslav Gordeyev, slim and dapper, is quite the opposite. A virtuoso also, there is more of the elegant *danseur* about him and the brilliance of his dancing is disciplined by the etiquette of the *ballet d'école.* The third, Alexander Bogatyrev from Estonia, is also an exceptional dancer. But this impressive trio, all about thirty years old, are entering a peak period, but will they, come the 1980s, achieve the stature of a Vasiliev or Soloviev or come anywhere close to

the triumphs of a Baryshnikov, their own age?

A very special ballet artist of the U.S.S.R. is the enormously popular and greatly honored (Hon. Artist of the Russian Soviet Federal Socialist Republic, 1964, Peoples' Artist, 1969, and Lenin Prize) Maris Liepa, one of the most versatile of contemporary Soviet dancers. He was born in Riga and became a student and later a member of the Latvian Ballet, but a festival appearance in Moscow as a youth brought him to the attention of ballet powers in the capital. He was invited to become a soloist with one of the finest and most adventurous ballet companies in Russia, the Ballet of the Stanislavsky and Nemirovich-Danchenko Music Theater (1955), and in 1960 to enter the Bolshoi Ballet as a principal dancer. Big, muscular, fair-haired, Liepa has excelled in roles demanding physical power and dramatic force, yet he has been able to assume the mantle of Albrecht in *Giselle* tastefully, dance the poetic male role in Fokine's *Les Sylphides* with remarkable lyricism, and to master the very special Fokine style of *Le Spectre de la Rose* through special studies outside of Russia and to introduce the Russian public to this Fokine masterpiece. A movie of *Spectre,* though unimaginatively filmed and with an inappropriate setting,

Maris Liepa in
Grigorovich's *Spartacus*.

Liepa in Fokine's *Le Spectre de la Rose*.

reveals Liepa's mastery of the elusive, almost spiritual quality of this gentle fantasy. It is almost impossible to believe that the same dancer could give us a Crassus in *Spartacus* almost terrifying in his savagery and towering, relentless evil.

Liepa, with this versatility and a vivid personality, has been permitted to appear in concerts, a very rare opportunity for any Soviet performer. He told me that he believed he was the first to appear in a personal dance concert since the ballerina Olga Lepeshinskaya in the 1940s. Liepa in these Moscow concerts attracted capacity audiences in programs in which he was assisted by his own pupils from his classes at the Bolshoi School. Among the experimental presentations were duets from *Romeo and Juliet*, with each *pas de deux* depicting a different period in the romance of the fated lovers and each accompanied by the appropriate passages from the Shakespeare play, spoken, of course, in Russian.

There are many excellent movies of Liepa, including a documentary of his career and performances in major Bolshoi productions. Original television ballets starring Liepa reveal still other facets of his theatrical powers. In one, he appears exclusively as an actor, and a very good one.

But the most magical names in Russian ballet today are those of two world-famous defectors, both products of the Vaganova Choreographic Institute and of the great teacher Alexander Pushkin, and both onetime junior stars of the first magnitude of the Kirov Ballet, Rudolf Nureyev and Mikhail Baryshnikov.

Nureyev, since his defection to the West in 1961, has become the superstar of the entire world of dance. The term "superstar" may have become a cliché through overuse but no other single word can describe Nureyev's position in the theater. His incredible career has represented not only the *ascendancy* of the male dancer but also his *supremacy*. At first, his name coupled with that of Margot Fonteyn meant sold-out theaters. Subsequently, his guest appearances with various companies signaled lines at box offices around the world. When he first decided to have a Broadway run on his own with a small supporting ensemble, it was as *Nureyev and Friends*, but this proved to be unnecessary and later it was

Liepa in *The Fourth*,
an avant-garde motion picture.

Liepa in *Walpurgis Night*.

Liepa, teaching in Moscow.

Alexander Godunov with Maya Plisetskaya in Roland Petit's *La Rose Malade*.

enough to simply announce *Nureyev*. Audiences for such Broadway runs were not composed exclusively of dance fans; it was the public that came, for Nureyev was more than a *premier danseur*, he was a total star of the theater.

The journey for Rudolf Hametovich Nureyev, son of Moslem Tartars, descendant of the Tartar hordes that swept out of Mongolia into Russia centuries ago, was born on a train as it swept, or chugged, from Mongolia and across Siberia westward. He has rarely stopped since. The living was harsh in Ufa in Eastern Russia near the Urals; food was scarce and two families were crowded together in one room. Today, he has limousines, yachts, private planes, and palaces at his disposal. The journey in between is a marvelous tale of luck, ambition, and talent, mostly the last two. At five, he saw his first ballet—his mother had managed to squeeze the entire family into the theater on a single ticket—and the future course seemed clear to the child. First, he joined a Bashkir folk dance group. Next, he studied ballet in Ufa with a former Diaghilev dancer. When a group of dancers from his native province of Bashkiria was going to Moscow for a festival of regional dance companies, among them the Ufa ballet troupe, Rudi was not invited to go, but illness felled one of the soloists and Nureyev volunteered. Thus, he got himself to Moscow, but Leningrad was his goal. He bought a one-way ticket. He was sixteen years old. No one at the Kirov expected him. He wasn't even wanted. But he stuck it out. Alexander Pushkin, the great teacher, saw him, took him under his wing, taught him, guided him. Always a maverick, always defiant of authority, always in trouble, he managed to finish his studies at the Kirov in three years and emerge as the best dancer in the school. Natalia Dudinskaya, the veteran prima ballerina of the Kirov, invited the teenager to partner her in Chaboukiani's demanding *Laurencia*, and the Bolshoi, the Ballet of the Stanislavsky Nemirovich-Danchenko Music Theater, and the Kirov all bid for him. He chose the Kirov and managed somehow to have his personal choice honored, possibly because of the influential Dudinskaya.

He was a sensational success in Russia—news of the boy wonder spread across the ballet world —and a sensation when, in 1961, the Kirov Ballet performed in Paris. This was the decisive moment. Young Rudi had done the unforgivable by enjoying the company of foreigners, by not sticking with the Soviet dancers, usually kept together for all social events, and eluding the Soviet guards appointed to watch over them. When the troupe was to leave Paris for London, Rudolf was informed that he was to return to Moscow to dance at the Kremlin. He didn't believe it for a second. At the airport, when the Russian guards were temporarily off-guard, Nureyev quickly moved over to two French policemen and asked for political sanctuary. At that moment, the U.S.S.R. lost its greatest male dancer; the world welcomed the man who was to become the most spectacular male superstar in the three-hundred-year-old history of the ballet. The historic date? June 17, 1961.

Early in 1962 Nureyev first came to America. I did one of the first interviews with him in New York. I was surprised at how well he spoke English but I shouldn't have been, for Maria Tallchief, who had come to know him well, has told me that he had studied English privately in Leningrad (although he was not supposed to have done so) and that he played the classics on the piano exceptionally well, an accomplishment that fascinated the American ballerina, who had made her own debut in a concert in which she both danced and played piano.

Between 1962 and today, Nureyev has changed drastically in some ways while remaining steadfast in others. He missed his family dreadfully. I remember him standing by a window in my apartment where we held the first interview and looking out as if his eyes would pierce space: "I talk to my mother on the telephone," he said sadly. "She and my sister Rosa . . . it is very difficult." Sixteen years later he was still hoping, backed by pleas from the world to Soviet officialdom, to get his mother out. He was mercurial then, as he is now. A smile well disappear in a cloud or, conversely, anger or gloom will be erased in an instant by a laugh.

I liked him from the first. As he became more famous, and more pressured, tales of his temper

and tantrums were frequent. Some, perhaps, could be explained by the fact that a poor peasant had suddenly become powerful and rich and that a spirited youth, controlled by a rigid system of government, had become free. We have never been close friends but we've been good friends over these many years.

But other things have changed. In 1962 he said to me: "I don't like to dance too frequently. Performing empties you. In class or in watching someone else dance, you receive, you are refilled. Yes, I like to dance in class more than on the stage." But fifteen years later, when I spent a few days with him in Blackpool, England, on the set of the movie *Valentino*, in which he starred, he said: "I must dance every day. I cannot stop. That's why I have said 'No' to invitations to appear with the San Francisco Ballet. It isn't a matter of too much to dance but not enough."

Today, he drives himself inexorably dancing with Britain's Royal Ballet, London's Festival Ballet, the National Ballet of Canada, the American Ballet Theatre, and with troupes in Australia, Holland, Norway, for "there is so little time," as he said to me backstage at the Metropolitan Opera House. It was a passing remark but it came suddenly in the midst of a casual conversation and then it was gone, and I thought of how years before he had suddenly looked out a New York window to a distant land with deep, but momentary, longing.

He has changed with respect to his repertory; but he knew, back in 1962, that he would. The timing was important. He had not yet danced with the American Ballet Theatre and I asked him what he would perform. "Only my own repertory—*Giselle, pas de deux* from *Don Quixote*, 'Black Swan'—for now. It would not be wise to experiment at the start. I should appear at first only in ballets I know well. But after the first appearances, then I'd be eager to experiment with new roles." And experiment he has, eagerly, profoundly, almost remorselessly. Ashton created

Rudolf Nureyev, standing at the barre.
Linda Vartoogian

Nureyev in Béjart's *Songs of a Wayfarer.*
Linda Vartoogian

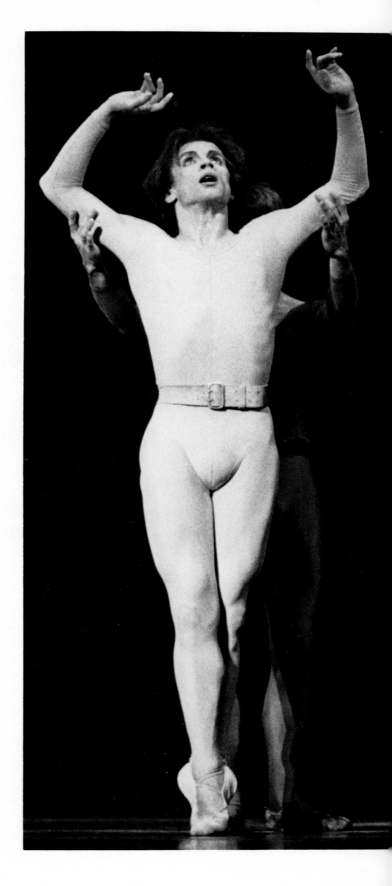

123

Rudolf Nureyev with Margot Fonteyn
in a scene from Martha Graham's *Lucifer*.
Martha Swope

for him. Drawn to Balanchine ballets but rejected by Balanchine himself because of his star status, he worked hard to master *Apollo*. He danced for Roland Petit, Rudi van Dantzig, Béjart, moving ever closer to modern dance until he came to the Empress of modern dance, Martha Graham, and like a beginning student mastered her technique until he could dance in her company not only in roles she created for him but in the pure Graham repertory itself. And then there was the movie *Valentino*, and a debut as an actor. But whatever the assignment, he has never deviated from the heart of a comment he said

that first time we talked: "Even an abstract ballet tells a story, the story of the body, *for the body must speak.*"

Shortly after his defection and following appearances with the Grand Ballet du Marquis de Cuevas and a London debut, partnering the American ballerina Rosella Hightower for a Royal Academy of Dancing Gala, he was chosen by Margot Fonteyn to be her partner. It was to become one of the great partnerships in the history of ballet. She was just past forty—she had always said she would retire at forty but circumstances altered her plans— and he was barely past twenty, but they were meant for each other . . . on stage. With his youth, his vigor, his impetuousness, his wildly romantic air, he gave her not only an extension to her career but also a radiance and a bravura she had never had before.

Nureyev in *Lucifer*.
Linda Vartoogian

He released something in her. She, in turn, gave him taste, polish, maturity. Together, they reached as close to perfection as seemed possible for two mortals. But then, they did not seem like mere mortals—they were dancing gods. Was there ever a *Romeo and Juliet* like theirs? ever a *Giselle?* ever a more passionate and poignant *Marguerite and Armand?* ever a more glittering *Swan Lake?*

There was the special aura too that spilled out of the ballet itself and into the curtain calls and over the footlights into the imaginations of audiences and columnists. It had to be romance,

didn't it? Just look at them together in the Balcony Scene and the Bedroom Scene in *Romeo and Juliet*, or at the curtain calls when Dame Margot plucked a rose from a bouquet, kissed it, and curtseyed low before him, raising her big, dark, lustrous eyes demurely to look at him. It didn't matter to the fans that Fonteyn was the devoted wife of a Panamanian diplomat and that she and Nureyev, although close friends, were hard-working, sweating colleagues. They would have none of that, for Fonteyn and Nureyev, Margot and Rudi, symbolized romance to audiences around the world.

When it came time for them to go their separate ways, except for occasional and nostalgic galas together, Nureyev then became the solo superstar. Of course, he danced with other ballerinas, some great ones, including that brilliant

Rudolf Nureyev and the Graham Dancers, with Nureyev
as the Revivalist, in Graham's *Appalachian Spring*.

Rudolf Nureyev and Diane Gray
in Martha Graham's *Night Journey*.
Martha Swope

defector from his former company, the Kirov, Natalia Makarova. But it was NUREYEV alone on a marquee, a billboard that sold tickets, that caused crowds of autograph-seekers and gawkers to assemble at stage doors.

It has also been Nureyev alone on stage or perhaps even isolated, or insulated, that gives one a sense of his power. He dances superbly with his colleagues and always has. This is not simply a matter of expert partnering but of rapport with his ballerina, dramatic, emotional, and remarkably kinetic involvement with those with him on stage. Yet his personal presence is so magnetic that he can, if warranted, shine alone. At the start of MacMillan's *Romeo and Juliet,* one senses Nureyev's presence before one actually sees him. There are others on stage but he is alone and he communicates, in some mysterious way, that aloneness. In a curtain call, he can stand, seemingly immobile, yet exude a power. Curiously, he invites applause simply for being there. Part of the secret is that he never really comes to a halt, for although he may be standing in one place, the stance itself is alive, poised for action, alert, "here." Further, whether he is dancing, acting, or performing in any way, in dramatic or romantic or purely abstract phrases, he follows two rules that he mentioned, not pontifically but as if they were obvious truths, as we drove through the night in his limousine along the Irish Sea from Blackpool to Liverpool: "Movement," he said, "should never falter," and, "There must be justification for whatever movement you do."

Rudolf Nureyev is forty now. Wisely, he is aware that before long, certain ballets, special virtuosities will no longer be right for him. He won't talk about it; like most dancers, he views age as a terrible issue. But he does not evade it. When he choreographed a new *Romeo and Juliet* for London's Festival Ballet, he designed the character and the dances for Romeo for himself as a dancer "for the years ahead." He has found the visceral virtuosity of modern dance, as distinct from classical ballet's virtuosity of the limbs, inviting and worthy of exploration and ballets with strong acting lines and/or modern dance influences he has realized are compatible and effective vehicles for him. In contemporary

Dutch ballets by Rudi van Dantzig, Hans van Manen, and Toer van Schayk, that triumvirate of resident choreographers of the exhilarating and adventuresome Dutch National Ballet, he has danced as brilliantly as he has in traditional classics, and in the avant-garde choreography of Murray Louis, he has astounded both critics and public with his mastery of movement styles, dynamics, body placements far removed from traditional forms.

Nureyev enjoys acting and found himself "pleasantly amazed" with his efforts as a speaking actor, but he will tell you firmly that "my first and foremost devotion is to dance." And he will add a remark that on the surface may seem vain but which, in reality, is a statement of a tremendous duty: "I am a performer, but most important is that I am a dancer. I *do* consider that I'm *endowed* with a very great talent and that is not something you can chuck around." The world of dance will agree with his appraisal.

Nureyev was the first Kirov-Maryinsky dancer to defect to the West since Alexandra Danilova, George Balanchine, and Tamara Geva left Russia in 1924 for a European tour and never returned, and since Vera Volkova, destined to become a great teacher, escaped to freedom in Shanghai in 1929 during a tour of Soviet dancers to the Orient. After Nureyev came another Kirov star, Natalia Makarova, in 1970, and then, in 1974 in Canada, the most electrifying virtuoso the world has ever seen defected, Mikhail Baryshnikov. Over half a century, the most famous ballet defectors came from the cradle of Russian ballet, the Kirov (Maryinsky) of Leningrad. I asked Makarova why she thought this was so. Charmingly, she noted that Alexander Pushkin, Russia's great poet-writer of the early nineteenth century, had described St. Petersburg as Russia's "Window to the West." Makarova then added her own words of wisdom: "So ve jump out. Moscow? No vindow!"

Another great, Alexander Pushkin, came along a century later and, as a teacher of ballet in Leningrad, trained and guided Baryshnikov as well as Nureyev. Pushkin, whom Baryshnikov has described as the last of the great teachers for male dancers in Russia, died in 1970. For Baryshnikov,

Nureyev in *Le Corsaire*.
Linda Vartoogian

then, there were two Pushkins behind his leap to freedom.

It may be difficult for Westerners and Americans especially to understand that not one of the trio of recent defectors defected for political reasons, except to the degree that politics affected their art experiences. And they did not fault their training at the Kirov and the Vaganova Institute. What they found intolerable was the isolation from the great dance explosion outside their na-

tive land. Their brief tours had let them see Ashton, Balanchine, Béjart, de Mille, Graham, Tudor, Limón, and countless innovators with new roles, new styles, fresh challenges, and all of these were denied them at home. More than they belonged to the Russia they all loved, they belonged to the world of dance.

Baryshnikov, born and raised in Riga, had his first excellent ballet training in Latvia. Coming to Leningrad, he auditioned for entrance at the Vaganova school and at fifteen became a pupil of Pushkin, who guided him for his remaining three years in the school and later when he had be-

Mikhail Baryshnikov in Antony Tudor's *Shadowplay*,
for the American Ballet Theatre.
Martha Swope

Baryshnikov in *Medea*, choreographed by
John Butler, with Carla Fracci.
Linda Vartoogian

come a member of the Kirov, joining as soloist
and skipping *corps de ballet* duties entirely. At
eighteen, he won the prized Gold Medal at the
prestigious International Ballet Competition at
Varna, Bulgaria, and a few seasons later the Gold
Medal for the Moscow Ballet Competition and
Paris' Nijinsky Prize.

Baryshnikov was very special even in his socialist, collectivist homeland. He had his own
apartment despite his youth and although he was
cast in traditional ballets for the most part, new
works were created especially for him. He danced
in Konstantin Sergeyev's *Hamlet* and Leonid
Jacobsen, one of the most experimental of Russian choreographers, created for Baryshnikov a
solo, *Vestris*, based on the virtuosities, style, versatility of the great Auguste Vestris of dance
history. But these were not enough for young
Misha, as Baryshnikov is called by his friends.

Pushkin had died just before Baryshnikov defected and Jacobsen, elderly, had only another
year to live. In Toronto, on tour, Baryshnikov
sensed it was now or never. He left Russia behind
him.

"I just don't believe it!" "It's not possible!" "I
must have been dreaming!" These are just a few
of the hundreds, even thousands, of comments
heard when Baryshnikov first danced in America.
Films from the Varna Competition of 1966 had
shown us an incredible dancer with a technique
of such magnitude that it seemed unequaled anywhere. Live, Baryshnikov was even more incredible. There were feats of skill, all classical, for
which there appeared to be no proper terminology. Yes, there seemed to be an example of
batterie, a *cabriole*, a *grand jeté*, a *fouetté*, a . . .
but what *had* we just witnessed? Every detail of
the movement was clearly etched in space,

flawlessly phrased, wholly classical, but whatever had transpired was a miracle and one guessed that it had never occurred before. The "Grand Pas de Deux" from *Don Quixote* had never, ever looked like that before. The physical skill of an Olympic champion, the total elegance of the ballet *danseur noble*, the fire of the Spaniard, the precision of a computer, the brilliance of a comet, all were combined here in this long-familiar, over-familiar ballet showpiece. One doubted one's own eyes. It just didn't seem possible. It was. Mikhail Baryshnikov was sensational.

The dancer himself immediately set to work to make use of that new artistic freedom he had sought. Of course, he continued to dance *Don Q*, he thrilled us in *Le Corsaire* and *La Bayadère*, delighted us in *Coppélia* and *La Fille Mal*

Gardée, touched us deeply in *Giselle*, and in all these traditional ballets continued to grow as an artist. But he stepped forth to dance Tudor's lovely ritual-ballet with fantasy and reality brushed with psychological tones, *Shadowplay*; he went slumming with vaudeville antics and burlesque comedian buffoonery in Twyla Tharp's *Push Comes to Shove*; he dug deep into his core of primal energy to dance Glen Tetley's *Le Sacre du Printemps*, and he danced for Ailey and Feld and others eager to create for him, among them, John Butler, whose *Medea*, a duet for Carla Fracci and Baryshnikov, saw him grasp the very essence of modern dance in rooting all movement motivation in the body-mass itself, in this case, the primal, sensual, sexual pelvis.

Did such movement come to him instinctively?

Baryshnikov in Roland Petit's *Le Jeune Homme et la Mort*, with Bonnie Mathis.
Martha Swope

"Not at all," he told me. "*Medea* was my first experience in this and I was lucky because my choreographer and my coach was John. He did more than give me steps. It was like going to school and learning why I did a movement. The Martha Graham influence in his dance was very strong and there was not time for me to study in class with Martha but our rehearsals were almost like a modern class with everything explained. Not teaching just what a step *is* but what a step is *about*. This ballet, of course, was a combination of classical dance and modern. The best way would be to go to modern dance classes for at least two months as preparation for such ballets. But there is not the time. So many styles in modern dance! It would be better preparation and more interesting to learn in class. But there is not the time for this right now. So I must learn modern dance at the upper level of instruction, through the choreography itself, without any foundation. I never did modern or jazz before

now. It is fascinating and exciting! I had only had classical, so it required a different physical and mental preparation."

I asked him if he thought that modern dance helped him, since he was already a fine actor-dancer, to convey dramatic or emotional ideas better than traditional mime. "Oh, sure," he said, "because in neoclassical works, in new dances it is not so important to explain a story or a character because modern dance is often fantastic in that it can explain deep and almost grandiose problems. Sometimes a Tudor ballet in one act says much more than a traditional ballet in four acts. There is something symbolic about such a ballet. Yes, it is organic, I agree, but it is also like telling fortune through cards, through symbols, and each

Baryshnikov in Act I (rehearsal) of his staging of *The Nutcracker*.
Martha Swope

person can read into them what he thinks he sees, creating his own image."

In Russia he had had "only a limited vision of modern dance, only limited experiences" in seeing bits of Ailey, of Robbins, of Béjart, and others, so when he came to learn new ballets it was difficult to do more than master new movements, to give them meaning. "With Albrecht, for example, I already knew the steps in the ballet—we have them in class—so I simply worked on *how* I would do them in that particular role. With my role in *Medea*, I had to con-centrate on simply how to do the movements because they were new and strange to me. Besides, it is not a story ballet; it is a dialogue ballet and very symbolic dialogue it is. Here between Jason and Medea is not the story conflict but the emotional conflict."

With traditional ballets, the steps may change slightly from production to production and this calls for variety from the performer, but Baryshnikov does, naturally, bring something of himself to each classical characterization. "I may think a step should be bigger or softer or different in

Two photos of Valery Panov and his wife,
Galina. One is from *Harlequinade*,
taken in Israel, the other a portrait.
F. Randolph Swartz

Baryshnikov in Act II of *The Nutcracker.*
Martha Swope

some way from the way another dancer does it.
It's how to do it. It's the conception. It's what
the role means to you. What is the sense of this
variation? What are the emotions? All of these
things matter.

"It is important for me now to work in all
styles possible. I could not be better than anyone
else in Martha Graham's style—I could not be a
top dancer there, not the same as in classical
dance where I have all my training. But the
important thing is to be a dancer. And to be a
better classical dancer, it is necessary to try every-

thing in dance because you'll come back to it better and stronger than before. I should be able to dance anything assigned to me, anything I want to do. That's why I need all this experience."

His classical skills, his virtuosity, and his very personal dance styles are captured forever in the popular film *The Turning Point*. In this movie he also added another dimension to his performing: acting. And with rousing success!

He believes that his new experiences have enriched his interpretation of the classics. "I have a feeling my first Albrecht would seem funny to me now. I'm not quite sure how I've changed but I know I have. I know also that my Albrecht this year is different from my Albrecht last year. But I knew from the start the symbolic purposes of the steps. His *cabrioles* are not just *cabrioles*, the *brisés* aren't just *brisés*, the *pirouettes* are not just *pirouettes*. This is Albrecht confronted by the Queen of the Wilis in this one scene I'm thinking of now. It is the expression of his despair. It is also the expressing of his requests to the Queen of the Wilis. And it is an expression of his inner being. A double air turn is a step. It is a beautiful step. But it should not be just a step. What is this step, right here, all about? Yes, I agree, steps should be eloquent."

Learning modern dance and modern ballet has, for Baryshnikov, "thrown light into dark corners. I have found faults with myself that I perhaps would never have discovered without these new experiences with modern. And I shall learn even more as I leave the ABT and join the New York City Ballet to learn all the Balanchine ballets and to be under the direction of Balanchine himself.

"In this century, a dancer should be a good technician, a good partner, a good actor, and he should be flexible for dancing in many, many styles. And I don't want to be virtuoso; I don't want to be actor; I want to be just dancer." In the case of Mikhail Baryshnikov, the word "just" has implications of staggering proportions, but it is his very simple way of describing one of the great dancers of the age.

Valery Panov, another Kirov dancer, also made international headlines, although he did not de-fect. In 1972 he had asked for permission to leave the U.S.S.R. and, because of a Jewish heritage, to emigrate to Israel. The permission was refused and, in addition, he was fired from the company along with his wife, the young dancer Galina Ragozina. Briefly, he was imprisoned. The dance world took up the cause of the Panovs and petitions and protests bombarded the Soviet officialdom until grudgingly, in 1974, it bowed to intense public opinion and permitted the Panovs to leave.

Valery, a brilliant *demi-caractère* dancer at the Kirov and seen briefly in America in a Russian music and dance highlights program in which he was praised for virtuosity and chided for hamming, was thirty-six years old when he was permitted to leave. He had not been allowed to attend classes and had endeavored to exercise within the confines of his and Galina's small flat. Thus, he was not in top dance shape when he first performed in the West in 1974. A stubborn, opinionated, and somewhat vain man, he did not take to offers of training, or retraining, help from major ballet instructors, preferring to work by himself. Hence, his return to a level of concert pitch was delayed and, because of his age, he never recaptured the total bravura he had had as a young dancer. Still, his personal intensity, his strength, and his athleticism stirred audiences. And, he and his much younger, very blond, and slender wife, as a team, proved theatrically effective.

Because of the very nature of Valery Panov's struggle to escape oppression at home and because during the two-year fight by worldwide sympathizers to secure his release, he became a *cause célèbre*. But without the cause, would he have become celebrated as a great dancer? Is it too late? Except for his age, he could be compared with István Rabovsky, also a brilliant *demi-caractère* virtuoso, who at twenty-one in 1951 escaped with his dancer wife, Nora Kovach, from Hungary. Their book, *Leap Through the Curtain*, told of their escape; their career in the West was itinerant, rootless, and, despite Rabovsky's electrifying technique, short. The Panovs, if they find not only a home but also a national ballet company in Israel, may fare better.

11

MAGYAR COMMUNIST PRINCE AND THE PRINCE WITHOUT A PEDIGREE

Royes Fernandez and Lupe Serrano
in Act II of *Giselle*.
Fred Fehl

Royes Fernandez and Lupe Serrano
in the modern ballet *Las Hermanas*.
Martha Swope

IVAN NAGY, in classical roles, is very probably the most perfect *danseur noble* of our day. He has the bearing of a prince, the gallantry of a cavalier, the walk of an aristocrat, the sensitivity of the poet. To see him, in his Act II entrance in *Giselle*, simply walk across the stage toward the tomb of Giselle is to see the essence of contained anguish. The voluminous cape, handled exquisitely, insulates the mourning aristocrat from the rest of the world. The tread is deep but not heavy, the lowered head is contrite but not obeisant; there is the vulnerability of youth in its first profound sorrow, but there is no diminution of the authority of station in the social order. Right here is the essence of Albrecht, of the ballet itself, of a period.

Ivan was born in Debrecen, Hungary, in 1943. His mother gave him his first ballet lessons when he was a toddler, and when he was seven he was taken to an audition at the Budapest State Opera House. Hundreds applied, forty-eight were selected, and, years later, only six, including Ivan, graduated into the *corps de ballet* of the State Opera. At eighteen, he won a Silver Medal at the

(Overleaf) Richard Cragun in an
action shot in rehearsal.
Mira

International Ballet Competition in Varna, Bulgaria, and one of the judges happened to be a great male dance star of an earlier day, Frederic Franklin. At that time, Franklin was director of the National Ballet in Washington, D.C., and so impressed was he with the handsome, blond, classical dancer that he invited him to be a guest with the National Ballet as a principal. The Hungarian Government gave him permission to go, a decision that proved fateful on personal, artistic, and even high political levels.

Nagy was an instant success in America. He excelled, of course, in classical repertory. I remember seeing his first *Les Sylphides* and being overwhelmed by his mastery of the elusive, lyrical Fokine style, of his ability to evoke an aura of evanescent poetry. Just as important was his first exposure to new choreographies, new styles of dance. At home he had learned not only from Hungarian teachers but also from some of the very best of the Soviet instructors; in America, his dance education expanded still further. Brilliant, with a devastating wit and a passionate nature, Ivan was exhilarated by the artistic opportunities the free world offered. Furthermore, he fell in love, despite a wife in distant Budapest. A serious knee injury requiring expert treatment through operations compounded his desire to stay in America. The directors of the Budapest State Opera were not willing to recognize his new prestige and offered him, upon his return, a *corps de ballet* salary. Eventually he was fired from the company. Soon, he made his decision. He defected.

The operation on his knee was successful. He obtained a divorce and married the National Ballet's ballerina, the Australian Marilyn Burr; he fathered two daughters, Aniko and Tatiana, and then, moving from the National Ballet on to bigger challenges, he joined the New York City Ballet for a very brief period and then, in 1968, became a principal with the American Ballet Theatre. With ABT, he has risen to a position of international prominence and extended his personal repertory to the point that he has become one of the most versatile of today's dancers while retaining his place as the great *danseur noble* of the day. Furthermore, his remarkable gifts as a partner have led him to guest appearances throughout the world as a favorite cavalier for most of the world's foremost ballerinas, Dame Margot Fonteyn, Natalia Makarova, Cynthia Gregory, Gelsey Kirkland among them.

Along with his Russian defecting counterparts, he has always said that political considerations had nothing to do with his decision to leave his homeland. In fact, when criticis have described him as a "prince," he will laugh and say, "A communist prince!" A photograph I have from him is signed, "from your Magyar Kommunista Herceg" (from your Hungarian Communist Prince!). But like many artists, Ivan is apolitical. Curiously, then, he made a move that was of tremendous political significance to the world. As a defector from Hungary, he was viewed as a traitor. He could not visit his parents at home, although Marilyn and the children, British subjects, could. When his father died, the Hungarian Government permitted Ivan to attend the funeral on a limited entry permit. He was greeted ecstatically by his colleagues at the Budapest Opera and, although Marilyn had been fearful of his visit home, he was permitted to leave as promised. Then came the surprise. In Washington, he was asked to come into the Hungarian Consulate to sign some papers "connected with your recent visit." He did and one of the papers he signed was a passport recognizing his dual citizenship as a Hungarian and as a British subject, and granting him a diplomatic rank equal to that of an ambassador. Never before had a defector from the communist world been so treated. A new era for artists of the world had been heralded by this move.

Nagy, an accomplished technician, is not a virtuoso in the same sense as a Villella, a Baryshnikov, a Nureyev. His leaps are floating rather than rocket-like, his impeccable *batterie* is shimmering rather than gleaming. For a while, he had problems with *tours en l'air* but he mastered this difficulty so that these demands are comfortably met.

The artistry of Nagy as juxtaposed to the artistry of a brilliant virtuoso such as Baryshnikov was made manifest when the two danced in back-to-back performances of *Giselle*. New Yorkers were eagerly awaiting the Makarova-Baryshnikov *Giselle* slated by ABT for January 5, 1975, at the City Center 55th Street Theater, but the miracle, unanticipated, occurred the night before, on January 4, when Makarova danced a *Giselle* with a frequent partner, Nagy. On that occasion it was a radiant pairing, for the two, as if by magic, became immersed in their artistic togetherness and drew the audience with them into that curious chemistry of perfect union.

When the performance was over and the two were taking their curtain calls, they looked at each other as if they were oblivious of everything else, as if they knew they had experienced a danced unity that would probably never happen again. The next evening's *Giselle* with Makarova and Baryshnikov was a brilliant occasion but totally different in tone and in impact. The indisputable brilliance of the latter could not erase the radiance of the former, for Nagy, in his own way, could equal any dancer in the world.

Outside the classical and romantic field (he's superb as James in *La Sylphide*, deliciously brash as Franz in *Coppélia*, and funny-poignant in *La Fille Mal Gardée*) he is equally impressive, even in works that are partly or wholly modern dance in both form and motivation. In Eliot Feld's *At Midnight*, the initial dance of agonized loneliness is realized with reaching movements, and Nagy does these not as a ballet dancer would in terms of mimetic gesture but, rather, as the straining reach of the body itself, a reaching from the gut and continuing into space far beyond the extremities of the fingers themselves.

Nagy's Iago in Limón's masterpiece *The Moor's Pavane*, a distillation of the Othello trag-

Ivan Nagy with Cynthia Gregory rehearsing Michael Smuin's *The Eternal Idol*.
Martha Swope

Ivan Nagy in Budapest at age 12.

Nagy and Gregory rehearsing *The Eternal Idol.*
Martha Swope

edy, is in itself a performing masterpiece, for Nagy invests the body movements, the gestures, the sequences of action with a remorseless insinuation of evil, of the act of surreptitious poisoning. It is a portrayal of memorable power.

Versatility? Adaptability? How does he approach the demands? "It sounds corny, or even phony, but your whole rhythm changes with each role, with each partner. You know, I dance with so many big, famous ballerinas. How do I do it? I have to be in love. If I don't love the person temporarily—maybe I could kill her before or after the performance!—then it just doesn't work. I must idealize, so for the duration of the ballet, I'm really in love with Makarova or Carla Fracci

or whoever. After all, the male variation is probably two and a half minutes—maybe I'd be a better dancer if I saved myself for that!—but for me everything goes into the *whole* performance." Ballerinas ask for Ivan because they know with him they will have not only his physical support but also his loving help throughout the performance. Thus it was that for her first *Swan Lake,* Gelsey Kirkland, so often paired with Baryshnikov, asked that Ivan be her partner for the all-important debut in ballet's most challenging role.

In preparing for a special role, Nagy says: "When, for instance, I do *The Moor's Pavane,* which is one of my favorite ballets, I look upon it as a real challenge. This is not Prince Charming . . . with lots of makeup I can be that! Ballet line? You're born with it, so my mother can take credit for mine. Because I know I have line and I don't have to think about it. But Iago. When I

told José that it was my favorite ballet, first he couldn't believe it and then when he believed that, he couldn't believe I wanted to do Iago and not the Moor. So when he said okay and ABT knew I was to do it, the dancers simply freaked out. They couldn't believe Prince Charming with his ballet line wanted to be Iago.

"I find now, when I'm doing it, I get ready during the whole day. I get tied into myself, I'm evil, I'm unpleasant—my rotten side, my alter ego, seems to take over. I'm not really conscious of doing this but I guess I have to get wound up to the part. Once it's over I'm all right."

With an abstract ballet, the approach is different. It isn't the character or the drama that must be conveyed, it is the musical side. "The music for MacMillan's *Concerto*, for example, is so beautiful that I just let everything be in whatever mood I'm in for that day. Sometimes you have to let it be how you feel—after all, I'm not a made-in-Japan computer! I can't turn it on and off! But the music itself puts you in the mood as it starts."

Ivan, now that he has mastered multiple air turns, looks back on the days when he had his troubles with them. "It was just a hang-up," he says. "In *Coppélia* there were lots of them to do in the Czardas but because I had boots on I thought of it as the antics of a silly kid. But in *La Sylphide*, with only three *tours en l'air* in my variation, I just freaked out, probably because they were classical and essential to bravura. I never was a bravura dancer like Baryshnikov or Bujones, but I haven't tried to substitute other steps —unless I had an injury—in the variations I must do. I can control air turns now but I'm sensible enough to use my best side and to keep to my own style."

Ivan Nagy with Natalia Makarova
in George Balanchine's *Apollo*.
Louis Péres

Richard Cragun with Marcia Haydée
in the balcony scene from
Cranko's *Romeo and Juliet*.

As for Albrecht's walk to Giselle's tomb, a moment in ballet that has riveted the attention of ballet students as well as eliciting sighs from audiences, technique is involved here but it is hidden. "You cannot use the ballet dancer's turn-out walk here," he says. "You'd look like Donald Duck. The feet here must be closer to parallel. When I studied at the Bolshoi, I had hours with Lepeshinskaya on simply walking and running. She taught us about even the littlest nuances in walking. In *Swan Lake*, the Prince has a walk but it is totally different. You have to feel that you're walking on top of the world. In the solo that is like a soliloquy, you never really get off into space but you're on top of everything. It is a difficult solo, very sustained movements, but when I'm on stage it is too late to think of technique. I feel alone and actually, as the Prince, I relate to Hamlet as he says, 'To be or not to be . . .' That is what is happening in my mind and my being when I dance that."

Whether Nagy or Nureyev dances this contemplative solo, it never gets the same applause as the variation with all the spins and leaps, yet it is much more difficult technically and emotionally. But this simply indicates that most audiences look first in ballet for feats of skill rather than expressivity. Ivan reports that he is much more exhausted after doing *The Moor's Pavane* than after four acts of *Swan Lake*. "There is no variation at all in *Pavane*, but you never let go one minute while you're doing it. The inner tension, strength, alertness are always there. In *Swan Lake*, you act all the time, but you dance and stop and there is always a rest. But now that I've done modern, I find the classics easier simply because I've built up stamina essential to modern dance performance. I'm on stage in *Pavane* for twenty-five minutes and, even if I'm standing still, I cannot let go that inner tension. It must be there."

By dancing with a galaxy of ballerinas, Nagy's own versatility and sensitivity are kept ever on the alert, for one Swan Queen is not like another. Partnering each ballerina is a wholly different task even if the role and probably the actual steps are the same. "Everyone hears music differently," says Ivan. "And each one phrases music completely different. I may hear a note on the violin and want to take a breath and make that the peak of the phrase, but someone else will hear another note. No two dancers are alike. It is absolutely unbelievable that the same piece of music sounds so different to each individual. Then, ballerinas can have not only different personal styles but different national styles. Margot is of the English school and she structures her performance on that style. Makarova will tell me that in Russia she held her arms here and I must place her there. And even if every step is exactly the same for two ballerinas, the way they do it is different and I must support each ballerina in *her* school, *her* personal style, and with *her* musical phrasing. Finally, everyone has a different body and each must think, 'What is best for me?' and so I must adapt to that. I must know from beginning to end of a ballet what they are going to do and what they expect of me. For each, I learn her way down to the last nuance and when I dance with others I mustn't forget which is which."

Dramatically, each ballerina elicits a different response from Ivan. He goes back to his "falling in love" on stage. "I must fall in love at eight o'clock and I play my scenes to a specific girl and my interpretation is based on the way she plays her part. Marilyn sits out front and prays that my stage love affair will be over when the curtain comes down! It's like tennis, the ballerina's service may be gentle and your return is geared to that, or she may have a hard and fast service and you respond in kind. Playing roles is like that."

I asked him about roles in which he does little partnering, such as *Apollo*, a ballet about a man. He laughed. "I guess then I fall in love with me! Actually, I love *Apollo* and *Les Sylphides* and ballets where I must move alone a lot. Here I have my reputation based on partnering, on being a nice guy, on adoring my ballerina, and I talk about my favorite roles and they all sound chauvinistic! But when those girls got onto *pointe* way back, they nearly put us out of busi-

Richard Cragun in Cranko's *The Taming of the Shrew*
with Marcia Haydée for the Stuttgart Ballet.
Mira

ness, so I guess I like to have my Apollo moments when I'm *it!*"

In works such as *At Midnight,* Ivan actually experiences the loneliness and sadness of the youth he is portraying; it isn't simulated, it is felt, just as elements of his Iago spill over into life. "I don't believe a fourteen-year-old girl can *play* Juliet on stage. Maybe she is one in real life. But the stage is different. You put on your mask, you put on the greasepaint, but then the memories come to support you. You must have suffered, or hit rockbottom and been emotionally—not mentally!—disturbed in life to project tragedy. If your own life has been always Hallelujah, Baby! you just cannot project emotional depths.

"Not consciously, but subconsciously, when you go on stage you take with you not only all your years of technical training with its accomplishments, mastery, aches and hurts, but you also take onto stage with you your life with its hurts and pains and depths and heights. It's an involvement between yourself and your role; it's a commitment to your audience. It is theater, but it is real."

* * *

I always wanted to be a prince but I didn't have the pedigree," said Richard Cragun, the American *premier danseur* of Germany's great Stuttgart Ballet. "For a long time it was very hard for an American boy to become a ballet prince. All the princes were imported in the days of the Ballet Russe and very few American companies did the great classics. Maybe Ballet Theatre was an exception, but you think of Dolin and Youskevitch and Bruhn in the princely parts. Also, I think, American ballet repertories were not interested in the traditional ballets and hence had no need of princes. The accent was on new choreography, modern dance. Balanchine, our strong ballet force, was doing new ballets, not the

classics. But I wanted to be a prince and an American prince!"

Cragun, born in Sacramento of part-American Indian ancestry, of which he is very proud, began as most American boys who wanted to dance began, that is, with tap. He was a good tap dancer but his teachers saw that Ricky had some special talent and felt that the discipline of ballet would be good for him. And, of course, he too wanted to see himself become a prince. At sixteen, he was far from home and in the land of princes, for after studies at the Banff School of Fine Arts in Canada, he went to England and began his studies at the Royal Ballet School, and won the Adeline Genée scholarship of the Royal Academy of Dancing. From there, in 1962, he journeyed to Copenhagen for studies with the great Vera Volkova. Just as he turned eighteen, he was invited by John Cranko to join the Stuttgart Ballet, where he continued his Volkova-oriented studies with Anne Woolliams, the ballet

mistress and a Volkova disciple. Before he was twenty, he was promoted to the rank of a principal and began what was to become a contemporary yet historic partnership with the company's prima ballerina, Marcia Haydée.

Cranko, who restored to the ancient Stuttgart Ballet a luster it had not had since the days of Jean-Georges Noverre two centuries before, emerged as one of the great choreographers of the mid-twentieth century. His bent was toward full-length dramatic ballets, although he created brilliant, innovative, and powerful short pieces. His inspirations, however, came not just from dramas, narratives, tales but also from his dancers and their special gifts. He never taught at all. He left that to Anne and, a bit later, to Alan Beale, another Volkova product. They did the training, Cranko the creating. But for his Marcia, Ricky, Egon Madsen (a Dane trained by Volkova and a dancer in Tivoli's Pantomime Theater), and Birgit Keil (the first major German ballerina of the

postwar period), he created an awesome array of great dancing roles. So much did this quartet mean to him that close to the end of his very short life he created a stunning ballet titled *Initials R.B.M.E.* (for Richard, Birgit, Marcia, and Egon), which celebrated their distinctive gifts separately and in lovely union.

Cranko's *Romeo and Juliet,* one of the greatest (and the absolute favorite of many) stagings to the Prokofiev score, has had many casts, and although Ricky did not create the Romeo role for Cranko, he subsequently became the most dashing and passionate of Romeos, ardent and elegant, for Haydée's Juliet. Egon, who himself belongs in the category of great male dancers of our era, often plays the role of Mercutio, and just when you are certain that no one can ever equal him in it, he and Ricky switch parts and Egon becomes a noble, sensuous Romeo and Ricky a flip and sensual Mercutio.

Cranko created that rarity, a great comedy ballet, for Marcia and Ricky, with a droll cameo for Egon, based on Shakespeare's *The Taming of the Shrew.* The comedy, approaching slapstick but never quite, was kinetically hilarious and for Ricky, Cranko devised some virtuoso passages that would give pause to Bolshoi or Kirov stars. For Cragun is truly a virtuoso. Once, he found himself having trouble with his double air turns. He couldn't figure out why, for they had always been easy for him. He went to his ballet mistress. "Anne, what am I doing wrong?" he asked. "You need more momentum in your arms," said Anne. "Give 'em a good snap." He did and found that he had done a triple! For a while, he could do triples but not doubles, until Anne got going with him on harnessing the energy.

Ricky had had some modern dance training as a boy and Cranko wanted to use this facet of talent along with probing the very deep, self-searching side of Ricky's nature. He came up with *Opus I* (to music of Webern), a remarkable study of a youth who finds himself alone among

Cragun rehearsing with Marcia Haydée.
Jack Vartoogian

many and who must explore both his inner self and the outer world in order to find his own lonely way through the labyrinth of life. He was honored by this role, loved it and still does. But he needed to be a prince. And as his opportunities expanded, he was able to become the Prince for Margot Fonteyn (in guest appearances) as well as Haydée in classical repertory and in Cranko's resettings of some of the traditional ballets, among them, *The Nutcracker* and *Swan Lake,* both with princes.

"When I first said that I wanted to see America produce a prince in ballet," says Cragun, "I meant it literally. We produce classical male dancers here. You can go to a Balanchine class and see the men doing classical dance, but on stage the repertoire has a place for the classical male dancer of today in modern classics but no princes! I simply wanted to prove that I could be not only classical but princely. I'm not talking about the steps. But how do you not look like a farm boy? how do you walk? how do you sit on a throne? how do you kiss a lady's hand? My dream was that an American boy, practically just off the farm, could be accepted as a pedigreed European prince within the framework of the accepted ballet style. And that's what fascinated me, more than the actual physical technique which is taught everywhere.

"To get where I wanted to be, a prince, I think John helped me most. He would say, 'Rick, don't think you can't be something you weren't born to be or that wasn't in your background.' So he guided me and I worked at it. The idea of being a prince is really even more than what it sounds. To me, it's a symbol of total theater, for it means that when you get into a role you're absorbed by the role, you become that role. And I've found that if you come on stage and do not convince an audience that you are a prince, then you haven't yet learned how to be absorbed by a role."

He discovered that if he could be a prince convincingly, he could find a way to be a convincing Romeo, young and impetuous and adoring, or a roistering, riotous Petruchio. At fifteen, he had wanted to be a prince and felt that it was almost

151

impossible. At thirty-two, back in America for a tour, fans found him believable in all of his wide variety of roles, but the biggest compliment for him came from Alan Beale, who said, "For me, Richard, you are a prince." And Ricky nearly fell over: "Here in Alan is a pedigreed Englishman and for him to say that the California farm boy was a prince, well . . . I felt I'd made it! Why did it happen just then? Because I wasn't *trying* anymore to be something I had never been; I *was* my role. Or maybe my role became *me*."

Cragun has his own philosophy about the artist, the person and the role. He says, "I think the ego on stage is a tremendously important thing. People ask when I'm doing a part, say it's Romeo or Petruchio, how much is the author, how much the choreographer, how much Cragun. They are all there, but I don't think you can go on stage and hope the audience won't see *you*. Hell, I want them to see me, me as Romeo and me as Petruchio. The word 'ego' seems to have a very negative connotation these days. People think they have 'ego troubles' and rush to a psychiatrist. But I think the ego is a force on loan to you. Your body and its characteristics are simply there. You're born with them and die with them, but your ego is different; it is, as I say, a force on loan. If you deny its existence, that's false, and if you push it aside you cannot become alive on stage. I don't care about adulation for the body and face of Richard Cragun on stage, but I feel that the force of that ego is essential to the role and important to an audience. It sounds metaphysical but I believe it strongly. *It's the relating of a unique force to performing*."

In this, Cragun, without knowing it, echoes Martha Graham, who will tell even the shyest, most insecure pupil: "You are unique. No one else in the entire world is like you and no one ever will be, for only you were born of the same parents and grandparents and ancestral combinations and only you were born at that instant in the same place, the same house, the same bed, the same sheets. Only you. You are unique." And, as Cragun says: "If you have an identical twin, he was born two minutes later or two minutes earlier, so each twin, though alike, is unique. The ego is unique and couple that with doing a role, giving a performance, and you are using a power that no one else possesses. And 'unique' to me does not have a definition of being better or best but of being one and only."

To be a man in ballet today is different from what it once was. "The prince in the last century," says Cragun, "was the consort. That was his role. He was important, but only as a 'presenter' of the woman. Today is a day of women's lib, but I sometimes think that when Rudi defected, he liberated the male dancer. With that liberation of the male, he has been abetted by choreographers who have allied themselves with the male dancers and created for them new and major roles. And Cranko, bless him, was one of the best for this. He said that Petruchio must be as important as Kate, Onegin as Tatiana, and so on. Even the ballet *Onegin* is the man's name. A hundred years ago such a ballet would probably be called *Tatiana's Dream!* It's a men's lib for ballet that Cranko helped more than any other ballet choreographer, but it led to equality on stage, to the celebrating of the individual, not simply the female, not just the male, but the being."

Cragun points out that the emergence of the male as a potent force in ballet has led some choreographers to minimize the female, sometimes to an extreme, and he feels that this can be an affront. But turning his attention to new productions of the classics, he says, "Today, the male dancer has new variations added to the ballets. The old neglect is erased. The ballerina role was so perfectly structured in these old classics anyway and now her role is equaled by the new position of the male in the restudied, reworked, updated ballet." So for Richard Cragun, being a twentieth-century prince in classical ballet is not settling for being only a consort. "I never knew what it must have been like in the old days when the *danseur* stood back of the ballerina for a career of twenty years and wondered what was going on out front. I'm out front for my generation of princes and I like it there!"

152

12

AS BUTCH AS BOXERS AND BLACK CLASSIC FLAMBOYANCE

George Balanchine has glorified the ballerina in his work to the same degree, although on a different esthetic level, that Florenz Ziegfeld once did the showgirl. Only infrequently has he been inspired by a theme calling for the male as the focal point, although, ironically, two of his most famous ballets in this area are also two of his most famous and lasting: *Apollo* (originally *Apollon Musagète*) and *The Prodigal Son* (*Le Fils Prodigue*). Both were choreographed for Diaghilev's Ballets Russes and both starred, in the title roles, Serge Lifar, Diaghilev's last, and favorite, dance discovery.

As the guiding creative force of the New York City Ballet (founded in 1948) and its direct forebears (the Ballet Society and the American Ballet), Balanchine has been a seminal factor in the development of ballet in America since his arrival in this country in 1933. As a rule, the male in his ballets was a supportive figure, present for partnering. The woman singly, or women in sequence for a number of variations, or women in ensemble—*Symphonie Concertante* to music of Mozart would be an example—were of prime interest to Balanchine.

His repertory had featured *some* male dancers.

(Overleaf) Jacques d'Amboise in George Balanchine's *Apollo*, New York City Ballet.
Martha Swope

Lew Christensen, with the American Ballet, danced *Apollo* at the Metropolitan Opera House; William Dollar, an accomplished American male dancer, had brief performing seasons with Balanchine and partnered Vera Zorina in the movie *The Goldwyn Follies*, with dances by Balanchine; and Jerome Robbins was given the New York City Ballet's revival of *The Prodigal Son* and Balanchine created *Tyl Ulenspiegel* especially for him. But these were exceptions.

Therefore, the men dancers of Ballet Society and the New York City Ballet during its first years were not virtuosi. Balanchine did not, and could not if he would, create glittering soli for them. Nicholas Magallanes, Francisco Moncion, Todd Bolender were not bravura dancers but they were essential to the company and to Ameri-

Nicholas Magallanes in a scene
from George Balanchine's *Orpheus.*
Martha Swope

Francisco Moncion as the Dark Angel
and Nicholas Magallanes as Orpheus
in George Balanchine's *Orpheus.*
Martha Swope

can ballet of that era. Magallanes and Moncion were superb in Balanchine's *Orpheus* and Magallanes' dramatic gifts and undercurrented passion were brilliantly used by Ashton in *Illuminations,* created for NYCB. But male solos or solo phrases in most Balanchine ballets made very modest technical demands on the men of the troupe. That is, until André Eglevsky was engaged as *premier danseur* in 1951. But Eglevsky came to the Balanchine company as an established star, as the great virtuoso in ballet on the American scene. But what of male star material from the School of American Ballet headed by Balanchine and from the ranks of the New York City Ballet itself? The first and best are Jacques d'Amboise and Edward Villella.

From the days of Eglevsky on, the New York

City Ballet has imported many of its male principals. Following Eglevsky, there were Bruhn and Nagy (briefly), then Peter Martins, Helgi Tomasson, Peter Schaufuss, Jean-Pierre Bonnefous. But the homegrown d'Amboise and Villella have become not only the New York City Ballet's brightest male stars—and, indeed, the only male superstars in the thirty-five-year history of Balanchine's American era—but two of the great male dancers of the day. Both have now passed their virtuosic prime and confine their artistries to roles suitable to their middle years. Do they have successors, non-imported, within the framework of the company?

Jacques, a product of the School of American Ballet joined the NYCB in 1950 at sixteen and had made a name for himself as a potential star by the time he was nineteen. Eddie joined the NYCB late in 1957 at twenty and three years later burst onto the ballet scene as the most exciting male dancer America had produced in a long time, if ever before. Jacques was given his first chance in the New York City Ballet by Ashton, who selected him from the *corps de ballet* to do the leading role of Tristan in *Picnic at Tintagel*, commissioned for the company by Lincoln Kirstein, general director of the New York City Ballet. Jacques was a huge success, so much so that Kirstein had Lew Christensen's very American, very butch ballet *Filling Station* (which in 1938 had starred Lew as Mac, the filling station attendant) revived for Jacques. Villella's first principal role was in Jerome Robbins' *Afternoon of a Faun* and his smashing into the ranks of the major male dancers of the period came with his dancing of *The Prodigal Son*.

It is important to note that both Jacques and Eddie were typical American boys, highly athletic and super-virile. To a public still questioning the masculinity of the male dancer, d'Amboise and Villella provided satisfactory and satisfying answers: male dancers were as butch as boxers. In fact, Eddie was an amateur boxing champ with a letter to prove it.

D'Amboise, big, tall, and with an infectious grin, was the model of clean American youth, the boy next door. Watching him in Jerome Robbins' *Interplay*, the viewer saw in him the very essence of the ballet itself, "play." In Lew Christensen's *Con Amore*, he played a dashing, amorous pirate but, again, you knew he was "playing." With the most open, engaging manner American ballet had ever seen, he added superb physical virtuosity to his dancing. Just as Eglevsky could "sit" in air, so could Jacques—all six feet of him—pause vertical in air with all the impact of a kinetic exclamation point. Big as he was in his teen years and early twenties—he slimmed later—he had an easy takeoff for his great leaps and a remarkably soft, unhurried landing. The *pirouettes* were multiple, very multiple,

The Prodigal Son, with Francisco Moncion.
Martha Swope

157

Jacques d'Amboise with Allegra Kent
in Jerome Robbins' *Afternoon of a Faun.*
Martha Swope

Jacques d'Amboise with the
three Muses in Balanchine's *Apollo.*
Martha Swope

but Eglevsky had coached him in both matters of *ballon* and extended spinning. Balletomanes noticed that both André and Jacques did not rise onto the highest possible half-toe when turning; to the contrary, the *demi-pointe* was very *demi*, thus giving the foot a broader base for balance.

But, as Jacques matured, it turned out that he was much more than the personable boy next door, much more than ballet's answer to the football player, although he was both. He developed

stature as well as height and when he danced Balanchine's *Apollo*, there was no question but that a Greek god had deigned to visit us mortals. Fine dancers had performed this ballet Apollo before and others were to follow, but the d'Amboise portrayal became, for nearly two decades, the definitive one.

Within the patterns and discipline of choreography bordering on abstraction, Jacques built, as Balanchine's choreography conceived it, a matur-

ing progression from the man-child in swaddling clothes through the youth exploring the world around him and the godling sitting in judgment on the Muses to the god ascending Olympus. This Apollo was both physically beautiful and spiritually incandescent. D'Amboise had joined the hierarchy of great male dancers with this portrait in dance.

Balanchine, always totally inspired by the female dancing body, was pleased with Jacques's technical prowess, his virility, and, very probably, that American athleticism he had explored in one of his earliest American ballets, *Alma Mater*, on football. Whatever Balanchine's reasons, the male dancer in the New York City Ballet received new attention from the master. There were more American-type roles, in knock-out ballets such as *Western Symphony* and *Stars and Stripes*. Balanchine also guided Jacques into classical measures exploiting his curious blend of elegance and boyishness and his very striking virtuosities. There were also very modern roles for him in addition to the romantic assignments—Balanchine's one-act *Swan Lake* and *Scotch Symphony*—he took over as successor to Eglevsky.

Choreography has long interested d'Amboise—*Irish Fantasy* is probably the most successful of his creations—but so too has dance education. His sons have studied ballet and when they were in their pre-teens, Jacques started some classes for boys. They were nothing like your standard ballet class, for Jacques was sure the youngsters would find strict *barre* boring and traditional deportment silly. So he had them pile their coats and sweaters in a heap and see who could jump over them best. From this sort of game-competition-showoff beginnings, he edged them into ballet. And, who knows, perhaps one of the tough lads who leaped over a stack of sweaters will become a *premier danseur*. One has, indeed, decided to make it official, for although George d'Amboise, one of the kid jumpers, has gone on to other

Jacques d'Amboise with the New York City Ballet in the Hungarian dance in *Brahms-Schoenberg Quartet.*
Martha Swope

160

activities, his younger brother, Christopher, made his choice, at sixteen, to follow in his father's dancing footsteps. Thus, Christopher d'Amboise, son of dancers Jacques and Carolyn George d'Amboise, became a professional dancer with the New York City Ballet the year that his father celebrated his twenty-fifth anniversary as a soloist-principal with the NYCB. Both appear, in certain ballets, together on stage. But there is as yet no question that Jacques remains the star of the family.

Through his teaching and through his successful lecture-demonstrations, d'Amboise built up a reputation as a trainer-pedagogue, a very American combination for an instructor. In 1978, he was rewarded on the educational level with an appointment as Dean of Dance at the State University of New York at Purchase, New York, while retaining his principal dancer duties with the New York City Ballet.

Edward Villella, like d'Amboise, has long been actively working for greater dance knowledge and more extensive dance experience in the public school systems and on the college level. He too has sought to make ballet attractive to young American boys (and to their fathers) and he has also stressed the link between ballet training and sports, through college residencies, lecture-demonstrations, and television. But Eddie himself was always an athlete and he literally came to ballet class directly from the town's baseball lot, where he and other ten- and eleven-year-olds played.

Eddie's sister was studying ballet and when Mrs. Villella journeyed with her from Bayside, New York, to Manhattan and Balanchine's School of American Ballet, she would leave her son at home to play ball after school. But it seemed that he was getting into fights, horsing around in rough and tumble games so much that he was strained, sprained, bruised, or lacerated. In desperation, she then began to drag him along to ballet class, where he sat impatiently while his sister had her lesson. Partly out of boredom and partly out of curiosity, he began to take class too. It was better than squirming for an hour and a half. He took class and he was hooked.

Jacques d'Amboise in
George Balanchine's *Stars and Stripes*.
Martha Swope

Once, lying on the floor of a studio at the School of American Ballet, he was spotted by Jerome Robbins. The lad, resting but stretching leisurely, glancing into the mirror, attracted Robbins' creative instinct as well as his eye. From this quick image, Robbins choreographed one of his most successful ballets, *Afternoon of a Faun*, a modern, dance-rooted conception of the Debussy tone poem which Nijinsky had staged as his own first choreographic effort in 1912. Nijinsky had seen the ballet as the faun of Greek myth. Rob-

bins' faun was the dancer luxuriating in his own movements, living in his own reflection in the mirror and experiencing a brief union with a girl, not as the faun with the nymph in the forest, but in a studio and in their danced reflections in that all-important mirror. Francisco Moncion was the first to dance Robbins' *Faun*. But Eddie had inspired the ballet and, when he grew up, he danced it.

There was, however, a hiatus between the boy ballet student and the adult male dancer. Eddie's parents wanted him to go to college and get a degree. Wasn't a dancer's career short? Was it dependable? If anything went wrong could he support himself? Those were parental considerations and Eddie agreed to the college provided that once he had done what they had asked— complete his college education—that they would not stand in the way of his choosing a dance career if he so decided. He had one year of dance and academic training at New York City's unique High School of the Performing Arts. Subsequently, he enrolled in a four-year course at Maritime College and graduated with a Bachelor of Science degree in maritime transportation. It was during these school years that he won his boxing "letter" and kept his body in ballet condition by doing a daily class that had been put on phonograph records especially for him by the great ballerina Alexandra Danilova.

Classmates, aboard ship, heard the records as Eddie practiced and asked what he was up to. In certain cases, curiosity turned into genuine interest and some of the lads began to do the ballet exercises with him. In 1957, at twenty years, he graduated and went immediately into the New York City Ballet. His first leading part, of course, was as himself grown up in Robbins' *Afternoon of a Faun*, and his first triumph was in 1960 in *The Prodigal Son*. From there on in, it was a comet-like career for Villella. Where Jacques was tall and boyish, with an easygoing manner, Eddie was small, dark, and very intense. He was, in

Edward Villella with Patricia McBride
in Jerome Robbins' *Afternoon of a Faun*.
Martha Swope

Edward Villella in *Donizetti Variations*
by Balanchine, the New York City Ballet.
Martha Swope

Edward Villella in the title role
in Balanchine's *The Prodigal Son*.
Martha Swope

movement, like a coiled spring suddenly freed. Jacques rose into the air; Eddie either sprang or, when a dramatic situation called for it, exploded. In *Prodigal*, his first great leap into action incorporated these qualities, for it was a release from the bonds of home and it was also an expression of angry, supercharged defiance.

Villella's danced portrait of the Prodigal was as brilliant a characterization of restive youth as d'Amboise's portrait of an adolescent god had been in *Apollo*. Not only did it contain the elements of restiveness and defiance and ultimate contrition, but it also revealed all of the degrees in between: the relishing of a new-found freedom, bravado, the tentative yet eager first-contact with an experienced woman, inebriation, discovery of infidelity, remorse, agony, lostness, the desperate plea for forgiveness.

Villella, even after the initial triumph as the Prodigal, never ceased work on the part. He refined and deepened the almost passing but key relationships with his sisters, his dance with the towering Siren became psychological as well as physical, his crawling return to his father's forgiving arms became not so much a defeat as a pact.

In the ensuing years, Balanchine created many roles for him, most of them designed to release and exploit his incredible virtuosity. Among these was *Tarantella*, a *pas de deux* for him and Patricia McBride to music of Gottschalk (arranged by Hershy Kay), a dazzling showpiece that also gave dance release to Villella's romantic, ebullient, earthy Italian heritage. The pace of the work exploited Eddie's *molto vivace* skills as well as always remarkable leaps, here space-covering and close to the ground as contrasted to the high aerial sorties in such ballets as, say, *Donizetti Variations* in which he dazzled audiences in the Soviet Union and earned for himself an almost unprecedented encore.

Earlier, when the Bolshoi Ballet was on its first visit to New York from Moscow, all young American male dancers were fascinated by the strength of the Russian men, by their one-arm, overhead lifts effortlessly executed as they propelled their ladies aloft—we had always used two hands here —and by the last-minute, split-second catches in which the male dancer would grab the female as

she hurled herself, almost horizontally, across the stage at him. I remember that Eddie and I talked about this Bolshoi male prowess instantly. I had bet American men could do what the Russians did. Eddie agreed. With Judith Green of the New York City Ballet as a willing guinea pig, we got a studio and Eddie and Judy tried the lifts,

Villella in Jerome Robbins' *Watermill.*
Martha Swope

drops, catches, with me on the sidelines coaching or helping to catch Judy if a fall seemed imminent. It was fun. And of course Eddie could do anything the Russians could.

In a very elegant vein, Eddie danced Oberon in Balanchine's two-act ballet based on Shakespeare's *A Midsummer Night's Dream.* The chor-

eography was created especially for him and
Eddie was remarkable in it. His swiftness was
used appropriately for a creature of dreams, the
king of fairyland, but here was the lightness of an
evanescent creature instead of the earthiness of
the figure in *Tarantella.* There were, then, the
key ingredients of speed and lightness necessary
to Oberon, but one more quality was needed, a
commanding presence, for Oberon was a king.
Eddie, despite his shortness, brought stature to
his part. He seemed to tower over his queen, Titania, and their subjects and if height was only
an illusion, let it be remembered that Oberon too
is but illusion.

Balanchine's two-act *Harlequinade,* with Eddie
and Patricia McBride as Harlequin and Colum-
bine, was a natural for the NYCB's two most vi-
vacious dancers, and in Balanchine's three-act
Jewels, it was only sensible to star Patty and
Eddie as "Rubies," red, rich, full-blooded and
lusty. Placed, as Act II, between the cool of "Em-
eralds" (Act I) and the glitter of "Diamonds"
(Act III), "Rubies" gave off heat. Eddie and
Patty endowed it with flash, too, and charged it
with gusto through measures that ranged from
pure ballet to something very close to a cakewalk
and, pertinent to the 1960s, the popular dance
"The Frug." This section of *Jewels* was set to
Stravinsky's *Capriccio for Piano and Orchestra,*
and Villella and McBride saw to it that caprices
and capriciousness of spirit—even to some surprise jogging—brought a special kind of luster to
this remarkable ballet.

There were near-melodramatic excerpts from
"Rubies" in a 1968 television special, "A Man
Who Dances," starring Villella. In the filming of
a live performance Eddie sustained an agonizing
muscle cramp midway and this section, where he
collapsed in desperate pain in the wings of the
theater, was kept in. The retention of this painful
episode was criticized because it destroyed an illusion. But it was kept, at Villella's request, because it told the truth about the endless work,
passing pain, grueling demands upon and dedica-
tion of the dancer.

The tensions and injuries touched upon in the
TV show were increasing steadily in Villella's
life. He was OVER-dancing and he knew it. Al-

Arthur Mitchell with Suzanne Farrell in George
Balanchine's *Slaughter on Tenth Avenue,* the ballet
restaging of the number from the 1936 Broadway show
On Your Toes.
Martha Swope

though d'Amboise made guest appearances with
various companies, as do most principal dancers,
Eddie assumed an incredible number of guest
bookings. He did not do his guesting exclusively
between NYCB New York seasons but would literally dash across the country between local performances in order to perform one night in New
York, the next in San Francisco, then back to
New York and out the next day to Florida, Canada, or wherever the booking had been made. He

Arthur Mitchell with Diana Adams in the *pas de deux*
from the Balanchine-Stravinsky *Agon*.
Martha Swope

never experienced jet lag because he was not in one place long enough to have a "normal" time. He danced with injuries, ignoring them, and this, compounded with fatigue from overwork, pushed his stamina to the breaking point. While still in his thirties, his career as a virtuoso ended—his body could take no more punishment—and the roles left to him, other than partnering assignments, were, ironically, his first starring part, the boy-dancer in *Afternoon of a Faun* and other roles that did not demand the vaulting leaps, the windlike celerities for which he had become famous.

Great dancers, however, need not be great athletes. Even at the start, Villella combined eloquence of gesture, great acting skill with his athletic prowess. In 1972, Jerome Robbins created his *Watermill*, a Noh-influenced ballet, for Villella. Portions of the public were outraged by this contemporary view of slow-paced Japanese classical drama, for Villella barely moved, and that portion of his public expected him never to stop moving. But for the majority—or theater sophisticates at least—*Watermill* was (and is) a remarkable theatrical experience, if not actually a ballet. As time, very slow time, is indicated by the waxing, the waning, and the waxing of the moon, the man contemplates his own life. He enters with heavy robes upon him, the accumulated materials of his life, and strips slowly to near-nudity. Then he watches as the young run restlessly by and an old crone inches her way along the remaining pathway of her life, as romance and fertility, formal ritual and solitary reflection enter and leave the stream of days. By his very presence, his unflagging concentration and an inner energy, felt rather than seen, Villella hypnotized the audience with this unique portrayal. The doer had metamorphosed into the thinker, not only in this ballet but also, to a degree, in a career that was leading Eddie more and more into choreography, teaching, coaching, lecturing. But the evolution, though rueful because of the inherent sadness of change, was not regrettable—in both capacities, Edward Villella had represented the consummate artist.

Under the aegis of Balanchine, the world's first black classical dancer of international reputation was nurtured. There had been great black dancers in tap dancing—that fabulous dance form invented by the American Negro two centuries ago—and in every style of variety show dancing. There were black stars of modern dance and, of course, ethnic dance artists who celebrated black heritages in African and in Caribbean cultures. But Arthur Mitchell, trained in ballet and modern dance at New York City's High School of the Performing Arts, a soloist in the modern dance groups headed by John Butler and Donald McKayle, turned to a career in classical dance with the New York City Ballet. There were predecessors among blacks in ballet—Aubrey Hitchins, Anna Pavlova's partner from 1925 to 1930, directed an experimental all-black (himself excluded) ensemble in a ballet, modern, and jazz repertory for a brief period after World War II—but Mitchell became the first black male dancer to rise to fame within a major ballet troupe.

He joined the New York City Ballet in 1956 and three years later was promoted to principal. He was cast, at first, in roles created by predecessors, all white dancers, and brought not only his racial heritage but, more importantly, his highly individual skills to key roles in Balanchine's *Western Symphony* and Jerome Robbins's *Interplay*. Soon, Balanchine began to create roles especially for him, and among those in which he triumphed and with which he will always be associated were Puck in *A Midsummer Night's Dream*, an acting-dancing part rich in wit, physical antics, and stunning virtuosity, and as the male partner to Diana Adams' ballerina in the superb avant-garde (yet classical) *pas de deux* in the Balanchine-Stravinsky *Agon*.

In 1968, when Balanchine produced for ballet his historic *Slaughter on Tenth Avenue*, originally danced by the first Mrs. Balanchine, Tamara Geva, and Ray Bolger in the great 1936 Rodgers and Hart musical *On Your Toes*, Mitchell was paired with the Balanchine protégée of that period, Suzanne Farrell, in the successful, adapted revival.

But Arthur did not wish to be unique for his race. So, in 1968, he founded, in his birthplace, New York City's Harlem, a classical ballet school for black children and, with Dutch-born Karel Shook as his co-director, the Dance Theatre of Harlem. The school was established in a garage and pupils came from off the streets of Harlem. It swelled swiftly to an enrollment of over a thousand students and the company itself, after three short years, made its official debut (1971) in a program at the Guggenheim Museum of Art in New York City.

Assisted by Balanchine and Lincoln Kirstein, the recipient of grants from individuals, corporations, private foundations, and government funding, it has grown into an all-black classical ballet company—with some modern, jazz, and Afro-American-rooted works in its repertory—of national and even international significance.

The Blackamoor, from the earliest days of ballet and of courtly fetes (when "black" Moors were imported from Africa to amuse royalty), was a favorite figure in royal extravaganzas—Janet Collins, the brilliant black modern dance artist made a delightful and elegant bow to this aspect of her ancestry in a Blackamoor solo for her concert repertory—but after more than three centuries of ballet, Arthur Mitchell brought not only new stature to the black dancer but a new dimension to the art of ballet itself through the Dance Theatre of Harlem, its school, and the brilliant soloists it has developed.

Among the striking black male dancers emerging from Arthur Mitchell's enterprises is Paul Russell. Whether or not he will become a major ballet star remains to be seen. But he has mastered the technical hazards of such showpieces as *Le Corsaire* and *Don Quixote pas de deux* and has displayed his versatility in ballets by Balanchine, Mitchell, Geoffrey Holder, and other widely differing choreographers. His achievements are all the more remarkable since he did not begin ballet training until he was nineteen, when he was a tennis scholarship student at the University of California at Los Angeles. His goal, however, was to become a pharmacist.

In high school, the young Texan was known for his theatrical bent. He played the piano by ear, he became a member of the band, and was voted the most talented boy in his class. So why chemistry? "Because it seemed to me to be a pro-

fession that would provide security," he recalls. "Besides, my parents wanted me to prepare for some kind of stable job. Otherwise, I was a real tennis bum. I played every day, in the sun or in the rain and if it had snowed I would have played in that too."

But one day he went to an amateur, on-campus talent show. "It had everything on it from bugle playing to . . . well, you name it, they had it. But in the middle of it all was a *pas de deux*. I didn't even know what to call it. But the boy leaped into the air and did wonderful things with his legs—I know now they were *cabrioles*—and he lifted the girl so easily. I had never seen anything more beautiful in all my life. I looked at it and thought it would be marvelous to do something like that. But at that time, I didn't think of being a dancer. Not at all. That came later.

"I left school and I left home because the chemistry didn't interest me and I felt that it was all wrong. My father, who disapproved of my quitting, had bought me a car, a fifty-dollar car, and I just drove off. I stopped and worked and saved and then went on. I ended up in Hartford and I did the same thing: worked, earned, saved, spent. It was a pointless cycle. And then I saw an ad in the paper: SCHOLARSHIPS OFFERED TO QUALIFIED MALE DANCERS. I said, 'Wow!' because it had a ballet picture in the advertisement. I thought it would be something to do after work, a nice hobby. I recalled the ballet I had seen that time at UCLA and so I went to the library, got out a lot of ballet books, went to my room after work and tried to follow the diagrams in a technique book. After two weeks, I thought I was ready for the audition! So I went to Joseph Albano's school and after an audition board examined me, I was accepted. Mr. Albano had laughed when he knew I had come with no training at all, but he took me. Boys are hard to find in the regional ballet area. I guess they'd take anyone. They took me. And that's how it began."

He worked hard, for from the very first class, with its intense body disciplining, he knew that

"I wanted to be a dancer." His boss at the University of Hartford Library was sympathetic and realized that young Paul didn't want to be a typist all his life. He permitted him to work part-time so that he could pursue his ballet studies. Albano also nurtured his young talent with wisdom and understanding. "He would put me in the Hartford Ballet company class every day because he knew I had to get somewhere fast, but he also insisted that I take elementary class every day too because I had to get the fundamentals right. It was a marvelous balance for me. Albano also made me take the school's classes in modern dance, in Graham technique, because he knew that this would be a good, quick, and safe way for me to get the stretch I needed, the turnout, because I could press my body and muscle against the floor. There in Hartford, my whole life was turned around. I was reborn. I had my own renaissance."

Joe Albano took the eager novice under his wing, taught him not only about dancing but how to listen to music—"I always had thought opera was just screaming"—how to see paintings, what to feel in different textures of fabrics for costumes. He gave him his first part as Uncle Henry in a Mary Poppins ballet and led him into ballet classics first as a Candycane in *The Nutcracker* and, before long, as the Nutcracker Prince himself. Albano had trained him well and he was a success. Next came a brief period with the Syracuse Ballet, a few performances with the Garden State Ballet, and a scholarship at the School of American Ballet. He hoped that from this school he would get into the New York City Ballet, but Diana Adams, who had given up dancing for teaching, told him that there were no immediate openings in the company and suggested that he talk to her onetime *Agon* partner, Arthur Mitchell. "I went to see Arthur right away," says Paul. "At our very first meeting he engaged me for his company and one week later I was in Europe dancing with the Dance Theatre of Harlem."

His first major role with Arthur was in *Agon* with, of course, an all-black cast. He enjoyed the Balanchine ballets but, as he says, "my head was with the classics. So I went to the Dance Collection at the New York Public Library and asked to see the movie *An Evening with the Royal Ballet*. In it Nureyev does *Corsaire*. So I saw the film again and again and I taught myself the whole thing by watching Nureyev. Later, I had coaching in the part, but I learned it really from Nureyev."

Paul feels a closeness to the great Russian classics because he recognizes a link between his own earthiness and that of the Russian dancers. "Their preparations for leaps and lifts are into the earth and I feel that too. I identify somehow with the big broad strong Russian style. At first my ideal was Erik Bruhn, but as I got more into this style of dancing, I looked toward Vasiliev as my model. I don't identify with British-style ballet. I have flamboyance, but it is classical flamboyance, and that's what Russian ballet is all about. And I don't think I can call myself a classical dancer until I have done the *Giselles*, the *Swan Lakes*, the *Sleeping Beauties*, and even *Romeo and Juliet*. Those are the ballets I must do. Perhaps I could bring something new to those old ballets, and maybe even to the new Russian ballets—my favorite right now is *Ivan the Terrible*."

Paul, very tall, very lean, very muscular, and very black, feels drawn to the Russian ballet and believes that he can bring something new to the old Russian classics and to contemporary Russian dramatic ballets. The "new" that he could bring, would it be personal? racial? He says, "Because I'm a black man, I have a different interpretation of what love is, and what hate is because of how I've been raised and because of the environment I have been in my whole life. There are characteristics, almost universal characteristics, of the black race that I would bring to a role, but there are also characteristics of Paul himself—me—and they would be there too. There are little things you feel that no other race feels, so if I were doing *Ivan* or *Romeo* or the full *Corsaire* I would, just instinctively, bring these bits of what maybe you could call race memory, but it would be the race as it comes through me, the individual, because I too feel things in a way that nobody else feels. Both would be there, my heritage and me."

13

DANCE WAS ALWAYS FOR THE MEN

EVERY TIME you come back to the *essence* of dancing," says Maurice Béjart, founder-director-chief choreographer of the Ballet of the 20th Century (Ballet du 20me Siècle), Belgium's royal ballet, "you have the male. Every time you come to *divertissements* in dance, you have the beautiful, soft line of the female. I think both are important because you need both on the stage, but sometimes I try to give more importance to the men because in the ballet the man has been pushed to the back for such a long time, he needs to make a comeback.

"I think now the dance is coming back to its original strengths. When you look at the prime civilizations of early times, dance was always something for the men. Still, in Africa, you see it is men who are dancing. In the vast variety of folklore—in the great Russian folk dancing, for example—the man dances much more than the girl. In Greece, you see the men are the dancers. And so it has been that dance has always been a virile activity. It has been only a hundred or two hundred years, when dance went from the people to the theater, it became a *divertissement* and the girls were what the elite wished to see."

Béjart, one of Europe's most popular choreographers and, to some segments of the American

(Overleaf) Michael Denard in a
French telecast of the *pas de deux* from MacMillan's
Romeo and Juliet.
Francette Levieux

Jorge Donn with Suzanne Farrell in Balanchine's
Meditation, New York City Ballet.
Martha Swope

Jorge Donn in the Béjart
ballet *Notre Faust.*
Jack Vartoogian

Jorge Donn in Béjart's
Nijinsky, Clown of God.
Jack Vartoogian

public, a controversial one, has not neglected the female. "I need both men and women," he says, "but I like to use one woman and lots of men. This is just the reverse of the old ballets when you had lots of girls and one Prince.

"I like to have a single girl be unique and surrounded by men. It is more interesting for me to choreograph that way. In terms of theatricality, you can make the stage seem full with twelve men. It would take sixty girls to fill that same stage. Of course, if you have a great ballerina, she can fill the stage by herself, but I'm talking about company choreography."

For Béjart, the "prince" in ballet belongs to the past. For him, the male in ballet is "a dancer, a sportsman, an actor. The male and female in ballet are equal but they are different. But there are androgynous elements in artists which interest me. I've done two ballets that touch upon the subject. I'm not happy with them yet. But I remember what Charlie Chaplin said when he was asked what he thought a dancer was. He said, 'A dancer is one-half boxer and one-half nun.' This looked at the sports aspect of dancing and the religious aspect of dancing. But notice, he didn't use the word 'priest.' He said 'nun,' so I feel that he meant in every dancer there was a piece of the other sex."

Béjart's most brilliant product in the male dance area is the Argentine-born Jorge Donn. For Donn, there is no allure in the traditional classics. "For me," he says, "Béjart is the complete choreographer. He is the best choreographer for men that there is." And Donn, with his beautiful body, as strong and as swift of movement as that of a boxer, and with a spirit and manner as gentle as "the nun" of Chaplin's description, has every reason to find Béjart "complete." The roles created for him draw from him the last amount of energy of the sportsman, the technique is that of a superbly trained ballet dancer, and the acting skill reaches across the footlights and invades the very senses of the viewer. One of the great Béjart ballets, a spectacle-biography, created for Donn is *Nijinsky, Clown of God*, and Donn is spectacular in it. "I could not be Nijinsky," he says, "because I am not Nijinsky the dancer, and in the ballet I dance no role of Nijinsky's but I dance my own feelings about Nijinsky and about myself and, I think, about the soul of Nijinsky." The result is a portrayal of such physical force that one is almost overwhelmed by the demands made upon a human body and of such passion and anguish that the tragedy and awful madness of Nijinsky stab deep into the viewer's very being.

In Béjart's *Le Molière Imaginaire*, Jorge Donn, star of Europe's most avant-garde ballet troupe, plays a part totally different from that of Nijinsky. He dances and acts the role of no less a dance being than Louis XIV, Le Roi Soleil, and so, ironically, an adventuresome, almost proletarian, mystical choreographer turns his attention to the gentleman who began it all, Royal Louis, and entrusts the role to the *premier danseur* of the Ballet of the 20th Century.

The twentieth century itself, as it enters its final decades, is producing the most technically accomplished and theatrically versatile male ballet dancers the world has ever seen—a generation of exploring, experimenting, experienced choreographers has seen to that—yet one finds that versatility and specialization go side by side. Donn, though totally trained in classical ballet technique, dances Béjart ballet almost exclusively and says he has no interest in the traditional ballets of the past. Russell, a black dancer, also classically

trained but with performing opportunities that have been centered in contemporary ballets, feels a dance identity with Russian ballet classics. Dancers of the New York City Ballet, classically trained, almost never dance the traditional classics within the repertory of their company; they must seek opportunities to dance the great roles of the past by guesting with other companies. Dancers of the Joffrey Ballet, classically trained, are exposed almost exclusively to a contemporary repertory.

Balanchine dancers, Joffrey dancers, Béjart dancers, and others enjoying membership in similar companies of contemporary orientation seem both content and artistically fulfilled where they are, but some of the most adventurous ones take time to explore their balletic heritage with companies such as the American Ballet Theatre, where past masterpieces and present dance challenges are offered them. Perhaps this is because the traditional classics provide a yardstick of judgment, of appraisal for the critic and the dancer, the audience and the performer. Generations of male dancers have sought recognition, approval, and stardom as Albrecht, Siegfried, James, Solor, Prince Charming, and others of that aristocratic breed. A soprano may enjoy tremendous success in operas by Bartok, Berg, and Janaček, but success in operas of Verdi, Puccini, Rossini, or Wagner can make her a prima donna.

There is no question but what Jorge Donn, in Béjart ballets, is a great dancer. But isn't it easier, quicker, and more certain to rate his contemporary, Michaël Denard of the Paris Opéra Ballet, as a great dancer? For Denard has excelled in Béjart's *Firebird*, as Siegfried in *Swan Lake*, in Fokine's *Les Sylphides*, and the reconstructed staging of Taglioni's original *La Sylphide* of 1832, in modern choreography by Merce Cunningham, in creations of Lifar, Tetley, Petit, Grigorovich, and others. Both Donn and Denard are tall and handsome, both have prodigious techniques, and both are accomplished actors in dance roles. Donn can tear you apart as he bares the soul of

Nijinsky in dance, but Denard, as Albrecht, can reveal the anguish of profound remorse in mime and in measures of movement that have the ancient eloquence that one would find, say, in Shakespeare.

The difference is that Donn, except for his classroom training in classical ballet, is wholly of the present. Denard brings onto the stage the accumulated treasures of ballet, technical, stylistic, even mythic. It is not that Denard is a better dancer than Donn, for he is not, but that he has a better showcase.

Thus it is, as new contenders come along seeking a place among the great male dancers of ballet, that we, the public and the ultimate judges, look for a measure, a rule, the yardstick, the criterion by which to rate the applicant. Is it

easier to judge the potential of big and sturdy Clark Tippett and small and slight George de la Pena because, with the American Ballet Theatre repertory, we can see them in *Swan Lake* and *Coppélia* as well as in pieces by Tetley and Tharp than it is, say, to grade the very real and gentle talent of Kevin MacKenzie in nonhistoric roles of the Joffrey repertory? Do we need to be sure that wiry, swift Kirk Peterson can do romantic roles in the classics, or is it enough to see him knock off with gusto the "Peasant" *pas de deux* in *Giselle* or do a loose-hipped Duke Ellington-supported solo in Alvin Ailey's *The River*? Does the fact that Robert Weiss of the New York City Ballet emulates his idol, Edward Villella, so strikingly mean that he will achieve great success as he matures, or that he will be only an imitator,

Fernando Bujones in
Jerome Robbins' *Fancy Free*.
Martha Swope

Fernando Bujones in *Don Quixote* *grand pas de deux,*
photographed onstage at Varna, Bulgaria, at the International
Ballet Competition where he won the gold medal.
F. Randolph Swartz

Patrick Dupond in a solo created by Max Bozzoni, onstage at Varna.
F. Randolph Swartz

Patrick Dupond being rehearsed by Anton Dolin in Act II of *Giselle*, onstage at Varna.
F. Randolph Swartz

and does the itinerant nature of Lawrence Rhodes's career from company to company in an amazing variety of roles mean that he is brilliantly versatile or unsure of his direction? When a phenomenon, however, comes along—a Nureyev or a Baryshnikov—we need no yardstick,

Patrick Dupond in the Foyer du Danse at the Opéra in Paris, being coached by Violette Verdy.
Michel Szabo

for they are beyond measure, they are unique.

Still, the balletomane is ever on the alert to discover the *premier danseur étoile* of tomorrow. And a great place to make such discoveries is where the yardstick is the scepter: Varna, Bulgaria, site of the International Ballet Competition, which did indeed herald the triumphs of Baryshnikov, Nagy, Vasiliev, and others of today's major stars. It was here that America's Fernando Bujones, a teenager, won the first gold medal to be awarded to an American male. From there, he has gone on to become a major star in the ballet world, a virtuoso who can probably match Baryshnikov step by step, if not yet in matters of flawless artistry, who can make himself felt as a true prince in *Swan Lake* as well as a

fierce yet vulnerable boy-prince of the jungle in Tudor's *Shadowplay.*

In the seasons immediately following the Varna win—for the International Ballet Competition is often referred to as the Olympics of the Dance—teenage Fernando found himself assigned to a position of increasing importance with the American Ballet Theatre and in demand for guest appearances in companies around the world. An initial brashness, touches of arrogance faded as the young dancer entered his twenties. With this maturing came a new sensitivity in the partnering of the ballerina, a greater command of princely deportment and of performing graciousness. The already dazzling physical prowess developed steadily, but as it did so, radiance as well as brightness, shimmer as well as shine were made manifest in his flights of virtuosity.

The Miami-born youth, trained in childhood by Cuba's Alicia Alonso and later by teachers at the School of American Ballet and the Juilliard School, is ready for the incredible variety of roles required of the *premier danseur* in these last decades of the twentieth century. Not only are his Princes now princely and his Cavaliers gallant but his command of today's dramatic dance creations and non-narrative abstract ballets is growing and in such enduring theater-dance masterpieces as the nineteenth century's *La Sylphide*, he interweaves the ardor of the lover, the dreams of a poet, the fantasies of the bewitched, the simplicity of a village youth with the élan of the *danseur* and the technical fireworks of a top-rank virtuoso.

Before Bujones appeared at Varna to win ovations for his dancing of variations from Petipa's bravura *Don Quixote*, Bournonville's mystical and romantic *La Sylphide*, and Jerome Robbins' earthy, American *Fancy Free*, he had been picked as a winner. His photograph arrived at the Competition offices in Sofia along with his application. A Bulgarian official told me, "We all looked at the picture and almost in unison we said, 'The winner.' We knew right then. We were right, weren't we?"

Two years later, another teenager, this one from France, walked onto the stage at Varna and everyone knew, even before he took a single step, "Winner!" For Patrick Dupond, barely more than a baby in dance, brought with him the presence of the dancer, the athlete, the actor. He was elegant of line and poignant of mien in an excerpt from Act II of *Giselle* and he was funny, spidery, and adorably antic in a new solo arranged for him by his teacher at the Paris Opéra, Max Bozzoni. The jurors, representing dance experts from many lands, and the audiences never doubted for a moment that Dupond, barring a catastrophe, would be a medalist.

But what looks spectacular on a teenager is not sufficient for a young artist in his twenties or the mature artist to come. So it happened that at Varna, two great male dancers of the past, each from a different generation, saw in young Patrick the material of greatness and they coached him. John Gilpin, a guest at the Competition, went to a rehearsal and taught him the phrasing for his solo from Harold Lander's *Etudes*, a ballet that demands technical and stylistic perfection and nothing more. And the great Anton Dolin was there to coach him with his Albrecht solo: "Your steps, Patrick, are all right," said Dolin, "but do you know why you are doing them? Do you know why you trail your left hand behind you as you walk in your diagonal?" Patrick did not know. "It is because the Wilis, unseen, are pulling you. Just don't hang your hand out; let us feel the tugging, the pulling. And at the end, what kind of a fall is that? Did you slip? Couldn't you think of anything else to do? No! That fall is the exclamation point at the end of a sentence of dramatic movement! It is all of your despair and grief and agony put into one final, shocking statement."

Gilpin had learned from Dolin, Dolin had learned from his predecessors back through Nijinsky to Perrot and before them to the Vestrises or to Noverre, the great master, who wrote more than two hundred years ago: "I will make an average man into an average dancer, provided he be passably well made. I will teach him how to move his arms and legs, to turn his head. I will give him steadiness, brilliancy, and speed; but I cannot endow him with that fire and intelligence, those graces and that expression of feeling which is the soul of true pantomime. Nature was always superior to art . . . It is not given to everyone to have taste, nature alone bestows it; education refines and perfects it; all the precepts that could be drawn up to produce it would be useless. It is either born with us or it is not. In the former case, it will reveal itself, in the latter the dancer will be mediocre always."

This is a book about dancers who were "born with it" and who "revealed it," great male dancers of the ballet from France's Louis XIV, the reincarnation of Apollo, to France's Patrick Dupond of three centuries later who was born with the gift and stands, as do young male dancers from many lands, on the threshold of revelation.

Walter Terry was born in New York City and raised in New Canaan, Connecticut. He first studied dance in college at the University of North Carolina, and was one of four principal male dancers in the student company. He has been a dance critic since 1936, beginning with the Boston *Herald*. He has since been dance critic and editor with the New York *Herald Tribune* and *World Journal Tribune*, and is presently dance critic for *Saturday Review*.

Mr. Terry has written articles for numerous periodicals in this country, including *Dance Magazine*, *Horizon*, *Kenyon Review*, and *Theatre Arts*, and in Europe for the London *Sunday Times* and *Politiken* in Copenhagen. He has done reference work on dance for Encyclopaedia Britannica and The Dance Encyclopedia; radio work on dance for "The Voice of America"; and worked as a scriptwriter, consultant, and narrator on television for both commercial and public networks. He is a dance consultant for such foundations as the Rockefeller, Guggenheim, and Ford, and for such organizations as the New York and Connecticut State Commissions on the Arts.

In addition, Walter Terry is the author of seventeen books on all facets of dance, including *The Dance in America*, *Star Performance*, *Isadora Duncan*, *100 Years of Dance Posters*, and *Ted Shawn: Father of American Dance*.

Walter Terry with Ivan Nagy at a rehearsal.
Steven Caras

Index